Dracula

Dracula: A Love Tale (2025): A Gothic Reimagining of the Vampire Legend | A Complete Movie Review, Themes, and Ending Explained

Johanna Grunwald

Table of Contents

Preface

Love, Loss, and the Price of Eternity

Some stories refuse to stay in the past. They return again and again, reshaped by the fears, desires, and questions of each new generation. *Dracula: A Love Tale (2025)* belongs to that tradition. It does not approach the vampire as a creature to be feared alone, but as a figure defined by longing—by the unbearable weight of love stretched across centuries. This is not simply a retelling of a familiar myth. It is a meditation on what happens when grief outlives time itself.

At its core, this film asks an old question in a modern voice: what does immortality cost? Rather than emphasizing shock or spectacle, it lingers on emotion. Love here is not comforting or redemptive by default; it is obsessive, painful, and enduring. The gothic world of the film—its shadowed halls, candlelit chambers, and vast historical sweep—serves as a stage for a deeply human drama. Eternity is not presented as a gift, but as a sentence. Memory becomes a wound that never closes.

Why does this version of *Dracula* matter now? Because contemporary cinema is increasingly interested in interior lives. Audiences are drawn to stories that slow down, that explore feeling as much as action. This film reflects that shift. It stands at the crossroads of romance and horror, choosing intimacy over fear and emotion over mythic distance. In doing so, it challenges expectations of what a

"Dracula movie" should be—and invites debate about what the legend can still become.

This companion book was written for readers who felt something while watching the film, whether admiration, discomfort, or confusion. It is for those who sensed that the story was reaching for more than surface-level thrills, and who want to understand how and why it does so. Within these chapters, you will find thoughtful analysis of the film's themes, its visual language, its narrative choices, and the questions it leaves behind. The goal is not to tell you what to think, but to give shape to the experience of watching— placing emotion, symbolism, and context into clearer focus.

Film lovers will recognize familiar gothic traditions at work here. Students and critics may appreciate the discussion of genre, tone, and interpretation. Casual viewers, too, will find guidance through a story that resists easy classification. Whether you were moved by the film's romantic intensity or unsettled by its excesses, this book offers space to reflect on both.

Dracula: A Love Tale is a film that invites contemplation as much as reaction. As you turn the page, consider this book an extension of that invitation—an opportunity to look closer, think deeper, and engage more fully with a story about love that refuses to die.

Chapter 1 — Introduction: Why Dracula: A Love Tale (2025) Matters

1.1 The Enduring Power of the Dracula Myth

There are very few figures in storytelling that survive repetition without losing their weight. Most myths thin out over time, their meanings dulled by familiarity, their symbols reduced to costume and gesture. Dracula has resisted that erosion. Instead of becoming smaller, he has grown heavier with each retelling. The myth does not simplify; it accumulates. Fear, desire, grief, faith, rebellion—all settle into the figure until he becomes less a character than a vessel for unresolved human tension.

Dracula endures because he is built around contradiction. He is immortal, yet defined by loss. He possesses extraordinary power, yet remains enslaved to memory. He defies death but cannot escape longing. The myth does not offer escape from mortality without consequence; it insists that consequence is the price. Immortality is not framed as freedom, but as emotional arrest. Time moves forward, but the self does not.

What makes Dracula persist is not his monstrosity, but his refusal to heal. Grief in this myth does not fade. It calcifies.

Love does not soften into memory; it sharpens into obsession. In that sense, Dracula is not a story about death, but about what happens when attachment outlives the world that once gave it meaning. Eternity becomes repetition rather than transcendence.

This is why the myth continues to resonate across eras that no longer share its original fears. Even as belief systems change, the emotional structure remains intact. The terror is not that Dracula drinks blood, but that he cannot release what he loves. He carries the past intact into every future moment. The myth survives because it reflects a fear that modern audiences still recognize: not the end of life, but the inability to move beyond what has been lost.

1.2 Why Dracula Continues to Be Reimagined

Dracula is reimagined not because earlier versions failed, but because the questions he embodies never settle. Each generation returns to the figure searching for a different answer, or perhaps a different way of asking. Is immortality a gift when it denies change? Can love survive without time, or does it turn inward and destructive? Is devotion still moral when it refuses to let go?

Modern storytelling has grown increasingly comfortable with ambiguity, and Dracula thrives in that space. He is neither purely villain nor misunderstood hero. His suffering does not excuse his violence, but neither does his violence erase his suffering. This moral instability is central to his power. The myth loses force when judgment becomes easy.

Reinterpretation allows the myth to remain alive rather than embalmed. Each new version emphasizes a different pressure point. Sometimes Dracula is framed as a threat to social order. Sometimes as a symbol of seduction and control. Sometimes as a tragic figure undone by love. These are not contradictions; they are reflections of shifting cultural anxieties. The myth adapts because it must. It is shaped by the fears and desires of those who retell it.

In an era less interested in monsters than in interior life, Dracula becomes increasingly introspective. The focus shifts from what he does to what he endures. Violence becomes consequence rather than spectacle. Horror becomes psychological rather than visceral. The vampire is no longer frightening because he is inhuman, but because he is recognizably human in his refusal to accept loss.

Reimagining Dracula is not an act of replacement. It is an act of confrontation. Each version asks what remains unresolved in the myth—and in us. That question does not disappear with repetition. It deepens.

1.3 Positioning *Dracula: A Love Tale* in Modern Cinema

Dracula: A Love Tale enters contemporary cinema with a clear refusal to resolve the myth into comfort or clarity. It does not rush toward horror as explanation, nor does it frame romance as redemption. Instead, it lingers in emotional stasis. Love is not presented as salvation, but as the very force that prevents release. The film's central tragedy is not death, but permanence.

This interpretation aligns with a broader cinematic movement that favors mood over momentum and emotional consequence over narrative efficiency. The story unfolds less as a sequence of events than as an extended state of feeling. Time stretches. Scenes breathe. The audience is not guided so much as held in place, asked to sit with devotion that has outlived its moral boundaries.

By positioning Dracula as a figure driven by love rather than hunger, the film complicates the romance it portrays. Devotion becomes indistinguishable from possession. Grief becomes identity. Immortality is stripped of its allure and revealed as paralysis. The centuries pass, but nothing resolves. Memory does not fade; it dominates.

Within modern cinema, this makes the film divisive by design. It resists the expectations of genre and the comfort of resolution. It allows beauty and excess to coexist without apology. Some viewers will experience this as operatic and immersive; others as indulgent and unsettling. The film does not attempt to reconcile these responses. It accepts fracture as part of engagement.

Placed alongside earlier adaptations, *Dracula: A Love Tale* does not seek to redefine the myth for all time. It offers a perspective shaped by contemporary concerns: emotional endurance, obsession disguised as devotion, and the cost of refusing change. What it leaves behind is not a lesson, but a question that remains uncomfortably open. If love refuses to die, does it remain love—or does it become something else entirely?

Chapter 2 — Creative Vision and Production Background

2.1 Origins of *Dracula: A Love Tale*

The origins of *Dracula: A Love Tale* are less about invention than about return. The film does not emerge from a desire to modernize the Dracula myth through novelty, but from an impulse to slow it down, to pull it inward, and to treat its emotional premises with unusual seriousness. Rather than asking how the story might shock contemporary audiences, the film appears to ask a quieter question: what emotional truth has been buried beneath repetition?

For decades, Dracula has been flattened by familiarity. His silhouette is instantly recognizable, his gestures predictable, his presence often reduced to atmosphere or iconography. In many adaptations, the character arrives already complete—fully formed as villain, seducer, or symbol. *Dracula: A Love Tale* seems to originate from a dissatisfaction with that completeness. It approaches the figure not as a finished myth, but as a wound that has never closed.

The film's conceptual foundation rests on grief rather than menace. Its starting point is not the vampire's hunger, but the moment of loss that precedes it. Love, here, is not a decorative motivation added to soften the character. It is the condition that produces him. The transformation into Dracula is not framed as a turn toward power, but as a refusal to accept absence. Immortality is not chosen for domination, but endured as consequence.

This shift in emphasis matters. By rooting the story in emotional catastrophe rather than supernatural corruption, the film aligns itself more closely with romantic tragedy than with traditional horror. The vampire becomes less a disruption of social order than a man arrested in time, unable to relinquish the past. The myth is stripped of its distance. What remains is intimacy, and with it, discomfort.

The decision to foreground love so completely is not without risk. Romance has often been used in Dracula adaptations as a veneer—an excuse for seduction, an aesthetic justification for violence. *Dracula: A Love Tale* treats romance differently. It refuses to frame love as inherently noble. Instead, it examines devotion as something that can curdle when it is denied an ending. Love becomes obsessive not because it is excessive, but because it is eternal.

This origin point reflects a broader creative impulse visible in contemporary cinema: a growing interest in interior states over external conflict. Rather than building the film around escalating threats, the narrative circles a single emotional fixation. The past does not recede. It repeats. Scenes echo one another across centuries, reinforcing the sense that time has become meaningless to the central figure. History does not progress; it accumulates.

The film's genesis also appears shaped by a desire to reclaim seriousness for a story often treated as spectacle. Instead of irony or self-awareness, the tone is earnest to the point of severity. The myth is not winked at or deconstructed. It is taken at face value, not as fantasy, but as emotional allegory. The result is a work that feels less concerned with reinvention than with excavation—digging into familiar material until something raw is exposed.

This approach explains why the film resists easy categorization. It is not horror in the traditional sense, nor is it a conventional romance. It occupies an uneasy space between genres, borrowing elements from each without fully committing to either. That ambiguity is not accidental. It reflects the film's central interest in emotional contradiction. Love and destruction coexist. Beauty and cruelty share the same frame.

The origin of *Dracula: A Love Tale* lies, ultimately, in a refusal to resolve these contradictions. Rather than smoothing them into coherence, the film allows them to remain in tension. It trusts the myth enough to leave it unfinished.

2.2 International Production and Release Strategy

The international production and release strategy of *Dracula: A Love Tale* mirrors the film's thematic identity. Like its central character, the film exists across borders, resisting a single point of origin or reception. It is neither anchored to one national cinema nor tailored exclusively to one audience. This global orientation shapes not only how the film was produced, but how it was positioned to be received.

The film's European foundation is significant. By emerging first outside the American studio system, it situates itself within a cinematic tradition more comfortable with ambiguity, excess, and emotional risk. European genre cinema has long allowed myth and melodrama to coexist without apology. In this context, a romantic, introspective Dracula feels less like a deviation and more like a continuation of an older, more operatic lineage.

The decision to debut the film internationally rather than through a U.S.-centric release strategy carries symbolic weight. It frames the film as part of a global conversation about myth rather than a product calibrated for a single market. The story of Dracula, after all, has always been transnational—rooted in Eastern European folklore, filtered through Victorian literature, and reshaped by countless cultures. The film's release pattern acknowledges that lineage.

Staggered releases inevitably shape perception. By the time the film reaches later markets, it arrives already carrying interpretations, debates, and reputations formed elsewhere. This delay creates a kind of echo effect. Audiences encounter not just the film, but the conversation surrounding it. Praise and criticism travel ahead of the work itself, influencing expectations before a single frame is seen.

For a film as tonally divisive as *Dracula: A Love Tale*, this can be both liability and advantage. The absence of a synchronized global release allows reactions to diverge rather than consolidate. In some territories, the film is framed as a bold romantic experiment. In others, it is received as indulgent or excessive. The lack of consensus becomes part of its identity.

This fragmentation aligns with the film's refusal of universality. *Dracula: A Love Tale* does not attempt to please all audiences at once. Its pacing, emotional intensity, and stylistic choices demand patience and tolerance for discomfort. Such demands are often more readily accepted in international or festival-oriented contexts than in mass-market releases designed for immediate gratification.

The film's gradual rollout also extends its lifespan. Rather than appearing and disappearing within a single release window, it unfolds over time, allowing discussion to evolve. Early viewers shape discourse; later audiences respond to that discourse. The film is not consumed all at once. It is revisited, argued over, reinterpreted.

This method of release reinforces the sense that *Dracula: A Love Tale* is not an event film, but a lingering one. It invites reflection rather than reaction. Viewers encounter it in different cultural moments, under different expectations, bringing their own frameworks to its unresolved questions.

In this way, the production and release strategy does more than distribute the film. It extends its themes into the real world. Just as Dracula exists across centuries without resolution, the film exists across markets without a single, settled meaning. It does not arrive to announce itself as definitive. It arrives to be contested.

What emerges from this strategy is a work that feels unanchored in the best sense—free from the need to declare itself a success or failure immediately. Its reception unfolds unevenly, shaped by geography, timing, and cultural context. That unevenness mirrors the film's own emotional logic. Nothing resolves cleanly. Nothing lands the same way twice.

In allowing the film to travel slowly and unevenly, the release strategy accepts that meaning is not fixed at the point of origin. It is formed in encounter. And like the myth it reinterprets, *Dracula: A Love Tale* seems content to exist in that unsettled space, carried forward by debate rather than consensus.

2.3 Expectations, Marketing, and Early Reception

Expectation has always been one of the quiet forces shaping how Dracula is received. Long before a viewer enters the theater, the myth has already prepared them for something specific: menace, seduction, violence, a familiar rhythm of fear and desire. *Dracula: A Love Tale* arrives carrying that inherited weight, and much of its early reception unfolds in response to the tension between what audiences anticipate and what the film withholds.

The marketing leaned heavily on atmosphere rather than explanation. Visuals emphasized shadow, intimacy, and historical scale, suggesting romance as much as horror. There was little urgency in the presentation, little promise of shock or momentum. Instead, the film was framed as somber, emotionally driven, and inward-looking. This restraint set the tone early. It signaled that the experience would ask for patience rather than adrenaline, reflection rather than release.

Such framing inevitably narrows and sharpens expectation at the same time. Viewers drawn in by the promise of gothic romance arrive prepared for slowness and mood. Those expecting a more conventional horror experience encounter something closer to emotional suspension. The film does not rush to meet familiar beats. It delays gratification. It lingers. In doing so, it creates a gap between expectation and experience that becomes central to its reception.

Early responses reflect this divide. Praise often centers on the film's seriousness—its willingness to treat love and grief as destructive forces rather than softening agents. Admirers describe an immersive atmosphere, a commitment to emotion that feels almost stubborn in its refusal to entertain easily. For these viewers, the film's restraint becomes its integrity. The absence of narrative urgency is not a flaw but a choice, one that allows feeling to accumulate rather than dissipate.

Criticism, however, emerges from the same qualities. Detractors describe indulgence where others see immersion. What feels contemplative to some registers as inert to others. The film's devotion to mood over movement is read, depending on perspective, as discipline or excess. Romance itself becomes a point of friction. For viewers accustomed to Dracula as predator or spectacle, the emphasis on devotion can feel like misdirection, even betrayal.

What is notable in early reception is not the polarity itself, but how rarely the film inspires indifference. Responses tend to be deliberate, even personal. Viewers argue with the film. They resist it or defend it with equal intensity. This suggests that the marketing, intentionally or not, succeeded in framing the work as something to be engaged with rather than consumed and discarded. The film invites judgment and seems to anticipate disagreement.

The absence of a unified critical consensus further reinforces this dynamic. Rather than settling into a stable reputation, the film exists in flux. Its meaning feels provisional, shaped by who encounters it and under what expectations. Some audiences approach it as romance and find it too bleak. Others approach it as horror and find it too tender. The film resists the comfort of alignment.

This resistance is not incidental. From its earliest presentation, *Dracula: A Love Tale* positions itself as an experience that does not explain itself fully. Marketing gestures toward emotion without clarifying intent. The film itself follows through on that ambiguity, refusing to reassure viewers that their expectations will be met. Instead, it leaves them with a question: not whether the film succeeded, but whether the expectations brought to it were ever compatible with what it was trying to express.

In this way, early reception becomes part of the work's meaning. The divide between anticipation and response mirrors the film's internal tension between love and destruction, devotion and consequence. The discomfort audiences feel is not separate from the film; it is an extension of it. *Dracula: A Love Tale* does not ask to be liked. It asks to be sat with. And the early reactions suggest that, for many, sitting with it is the most difficult—and revealing—part of the experience.

Chapter 3 — Story Overview (Spoiler-Free)

3.1 Narrative Premise and Setting

The narrative premise of *Dracula: A Love Tale* is deceptively simple, almost austere. A man loses the person who gives his life meaning, and time does not soften the loss. Instead, it stretches it. Centuries pass, civilizations rise and fall, yet the emotional moment that defines him remains intact. The story does not unfold as a quest in the traditional sense, but as a prolonged state of waiting—waiting for recognition, for return, for relief that never quite arrives.

The setting reflects this emotional suspension. History is not presented as progress, but as accumulation. The medieval past does not disappear when the story moves forward in time; it lingers, pressing against later centuries like a memory that refuses to fade. Castles, churches, and cities are not merely locations but containers of feeling. Stone remembers. Walls absorb devotion and violence alike. The physical world becomes an extension of the character's inner condition—grand, decaying, and heavy with what has been endured.

Rather than anchoring itself in a single moment, the film allows time to feel elastic. Centuries compress and expand according to emotional intensity rather than chronology. The past intrudes on the present without warning. The setting does not advance the narrative so much as echo it. Each era feels less like a new chapter and more like a variation on the same unresolved state.

This approach resists the comfort of historical clarity. The audience is not guided through time with firm markers or reassuring context. Instead, the film allows disorientation to persist. That disorientation mirrors the central condition of immortality as the film imagines it: an existence without temporal relief. When nothing ends, nothing truly begins either.

The world of *Dracula: A Love Tale* is therefore not a backdrop but a pressure. It weighs on the story rather than supporting it. Beauty and decay exist side by side, often in the same frame. Grandeur is inseparable from emptiness. The setting does not promise escape or renewal; it reinforces the sense that the past is inescapable, and that memory has more authority than the present moment.

In choosing this kind of setting, the film aligns itself with gothic tradition while quietly subverting it. The familiar elements—dark architecture, religious imagery, historical sweep—are not used to heighten fear, but to deepen stillness. The threat is not what lurks in the shadows, but what refuses to leave them.

3.2 Character Foundations and Central Conflict

The foundation of the film's central character is not built on hunger or ambition, but on attachment. Before the transformation into Dracula carries any supernatural weight, it is rooted in an emotional decision: the refusal to accept loss as final. This refusal becomes the defining act, more consequential than any curse or ritual. What follows is not a descent into monstrosity, but a long entrapment within a single feeling.

The character is shaped less by what he seeks than by what he cannot relinquish. Love, once severed by death, does not evolve into memory or mourning. It becomes fixed. Identity forms around it. Everything else—power, immortality, violence—feels secondary, almost incidental. The film presents these elements not as temptations but as byproducts of emotional paralysis.

This framing complicates the central conflict. There is no clear external antagonist that can be defeated to restore balance. The conflict exists within the character's relationship to time and devotion. Immortality does not liberate him from grief; it preserves it in perfect condition. Each century becomes another confirmation that nothing has changed, and that nothing will unless he allows it to.

Other characters enter the narrative not as equals, but as disruptions. They represent movement, mortality, and moral limits. Some confront him with judgment, others with desire, others with faith. Yet none of these encounters fully dislodge him from his fixation. Relationships do not develop so much as collide. Human connection brushes against something that no longer moves at a human pace.

What emerges is a conflict that resists resolution. The character is not torn between good and evil in any conventional sense. He is torn between continuation and release. To let go would mean accepting death, not just of another person, but of the self that has been constructed around loss. To persist means repeating harm, knowingly, indefinitely.

This is where the film's moral complexity sharpens. The character's suffering is real, but so is the damage he causes. The narrative does not attempt to balance these truths into equivalence. It allows them to exist simultaneously. Sympathy is possible, but never comfortable. Condemnation feels insufficient. The viewer is left in a position of ethical unease, unable to resolve the character into a single category.

The central conflict, then, is not whether Dracula can be stopped, redeemed, or destroyed. It is whether love that refuses to end can remain love at all. The film does not rush to answer this. It allows the question to deepen as the story progresses, pressing closer to the uncomfortable possibility that devotion, when stripped of finitude, may become its own form of violence.

3.3 Tone, Pacing, and First Impressions

The first impression of *Dracula: A Love Tale* is not one of urgency, but of suspension. The film does not announce itself through shock or momentum. It settles. From its opening moments, there is a sense that time will not behave normally here. Scenes arrive without haste and leave without resolution. The tone is measured, somber, and deliberate, as though the story itself is hesitant to move forward.

This restraint shapes the viewing experience immediately. The film asks for attention rather than excitement. Its emotional register is low and sustained, rarely spiking into overt spectacle. When violence or passion appears, it does not rupture the atmosphere so much as fold back into it. Nothing feels isolated. Everything belongs to the same continuous mood. The effect can feel immersive or suffocating, depending on the viewer's tolerance for stillness.

Pacing becomes an extension of character psychology. The slowness is not ornamental; it reflects an existence unmoored from urgency. Immortality, as imagined here, does not accelerate experience—it dilates it. Moments stretch because there is no deadline. The absence of forward momentum mirrors a life in which nothing ends. This is not a narrative that builds toward release. It circles.

For some viewers, this pacing produces an immediate sense of gravity. The film's patience allows emotion to accumulate quietly, without instruction. The audience is given space to observe, to linger, to sit with expressions and silences that would be hurried past in a more conventional structure. The stillness invites interpretation rather than reaction.

For others, the same qualities register as resistance. The lack of narrative propulsion can feel withholding. Expectations shaped by genre—anticipation of threat, escalation, or catharsis—are delayed or denied. The film does not reassure the viewer that their patience will be rewarded in familiar ways. It does not promise a payoff proportional to time invested.

Tone, in this context, becomes a form of argument. The film seems to insist that devotion, grief, and obsession are not experiences that move quickly or resolve cleanly. To pace the story briskly would be to misrepresent its subject. Emotional endurance demands endurance from the viewer as well.

First impressions, then, tend to harden quickly. Some viewers sense almost immediately that the film is operating on a different wavelength, and surrender to it. Others feel alienated within the first act, unsettled by the refusal to clarify intent or accelerate movement. These reactions are not misunderstandings. They are responses to a work that does not attempt to neutralize its own severity.

What remains striking is the film's confidence in this approach. It does not appear anxious about being misunderstood. It allows silence to linger. It permits repetition. It trusts that tone itself can carry meaning, even when events do not advance. The mood does not explain the story; it becomes the story.

By the end of the opening movement, the viewer has already been positioned. Not through exposition or promise, but through experience. The film has asked a quiet question: are you willing to remain here, in this emotional weather, without assurance of relief? The answer to that question often determines everything that follows.

Chapter 4 — Genre and Atmosphere

4.1 Gothic Romance Versus Traditional Horror

Dracula: A Love Tale positions itself uneasily between two traditions that share a long history but rarely coexist without tension. Traditional horror depends on rupture—on intrusion, shock, and the violation of boundaries. Gothic romance, by contrast, lingers. It is concerned less with fear than with atmosphere, less with threat than with emotional excess. This film chooses the latter without fully abandoning the former, and in doing so creates a persistent sense of unease that is not rooted in terror but in intimacy.

The absence of conventional horror rhythms is immediately apparent. There is little interest in suspense as escalation, little effort to build toward moments designed to frighten. Violence appears, but it does not arrive as spectacle. It emerges quietly, often as consequence rather than event. The film seems uninterested in startling the audience; it prefers to unsettle them by proximity. Horror, here, is not something that jumps out from the dark. It sits in the room.

Gothic romance allows the story to remain close to its central emotion without interruption. Love is not a reprieve from darkness but its deepest source. The film treats devotion as something vast and consuming, capable of shaping centuries without diminishing. This reframing alters the moral landscape. Fear gives way to discomfort. The question is no longer what Dracula will do, but what his love permits him to justify.

Traditional horror often offers release. Tension builds, then breaks. The monster is confronted, exposed, or destroyed. *Dracula: A Love Tale* resists that structure. There is no clean line between predator and victim, no moment where the audience is invited to feel safe in judgment. By aligning itself more closely with gothic romance, the film accepts emotional excess as its core condition. The danger lies not in sudden acts, but in the refusal of limits.

This choice narrows the distance between viewer and subject. Rather than positioning Dracula as an external threat, the film draws him inward, closer to the audience's own experiences of attachment and loss. The horror becomes reflective. It asks not what we fear, but what we might cling to beyond reason. In doing so, it sacrifices immediacy for depth, shock for persistence.

The result is a work that unsettles without alarming, that disturbs without announcing itself as disturbance. It does not seek to redefine horror, but to bypass it—using the language of romance to expose something equally disquieting. Love, when granted eternity, ceases to be comforting. It becomes absolute. And absolutes, the film suggests, are where danger truly begins.

4.2 Mood, Symbolism, and Visual Language

Mood in *Dracula: A Love Tale* is not decorative. It is structural. The film's emotional tone does not accompany the story; it determines how the story exists. Everything within the frame seems arranged to sustain a single atmosphere—heavy, reverent, and unrelieved. Light is scarce, movement restrained. The world appears to breathe slowly, as if conserving energy for an eternity it knows will never end.

Symbolism operates quietly, without insistence. Religious imagery appears not as doctrine but as pressure. Crosses, altars, and sacred spaces are present, yet they do not offer sanctuary. They function instead as reminders of judgment deferred rather than delivered. Faith lingers as absence, not comfort. The sacred is close, but unreachable. This distance mirrors the emotional separation at the heart of the film: devotion without communion, belief without resolution.

Architecture carries much of the film's meaning. Stone walls, vast interiors, and decaying grandeur do not simply establish period or genre. They externalize inner states. The weight of buildings reflects the weight of memory. Space feels both expansive and claustrophobic, suggesting an existence that stretches endlessly while remaining trapped within a single emotional frame.

The visual language favors stillness over motion. The camera often observes rather than pursues, allowing figures to remain small within their surroundings. When movement occurs, it feels deliberate, almost ceremonial. Nothing appears accidental. This controlled aesthetic reinforces the sense that life has hardened into ritual. Action becomes repetition. Gesture replaces urgency.

Color is subdued, rarely allowed to break the dominant palette of shadow and muted tones. When warmth appears, it feels fragile, temporary. Beauty is present, but it does not promise relief. It exists alongside decay, inseparable from it. The film seems uninterested in contrast as resolution. Light does not defeat darkness; it merely reveals it.

What emerges from this visual approach is a language that speaks less through explanation than through accumulation. Meaning gathers slowly, through repetition and restraint. Symbols are not pointed out; they are allowed to sit, unanswered. The viewer is invited to read the frame the way one reads a memory—imperfectly, emotionally, without certainty.

This commitment to mood over clarity demands patience. It also demands participation. The film does not decode itself. It offers images, rhythms, and spaces charged with feeling, then steps back. The effect is not instructive, but immersive. One does not watch the film so much as remain within it, absorbing its emotional climate.

In this visual world, nothing resolves. Symbols do not close into meaning. Mood does not lift. The film allows its language to remain open, unresolved, and heavy—much like the love it portrays. The question it leaves behind is not what any single image signifies, but whether immersion itself becomes a form of surrender.

4.3 How Atmosphere Shapes Audience Expectations

Atmosphere, in *Dracula: A Love Tale*, does not wait to be understood. It arrives first, quietly establishing the terms of engagement before the viewer has time to form clear expectations. Long before the narrative asserts itself, the film has already communicated what kind of experience it intends to be. This communication is not verbal or explicit. It is felt. And once felt, it is difficult to ignore.

The atmosphere signals restraint. It suggests that answers will not come quickly, if at all. This immediately places the viewer in a position of uncertainty. Familiar genre markers—anticipation of shock, rhythm of suspense, promise of release—begin to feel unreliable. The film does not announce that it will deny these pleasures; it simply withholds them. Expectations formed through habit encounter resistance, and the viewer must decide whether to adjust or withdraw.

For some, this atmosphere recalibrates attention. The absence of urgency encourages a different kind of watching—one that notices silence, posture, the weight of space between words. The viewer begins to expect meaning to emerge gradually, through accumulation rather than revelation. Emotion becomes something to be inferred rather than delivered. The film teaches its audience how to watch it by refusing to meet them halfway.

For others, the same atmosphere produces frustration. The lack of conventional signals can feel evasive, even hostile. When a film declines to clarify its intentions early, it risks alienating viewers who rely on expectation as orientation. The atmosphere does not reassure. It does not explain itself. It remains firm in its tone, indifferent to whether it is understood or accepted.

This indifference is crucial. The film does not adapt to its audience; it asks the audience to adapt to it. Atmosphere becomes a form of authorship, asserting control over pace, attention, and emotional response. The viewer is not guided so much as positioned. Expectations are shaped not through promise, but through pressure.

Over time, this pressure alters perception. What initially feels slow begins to feel deliberate. What seems withholding begins to feel precise. Or, conversely, what first appears contemplative hardens into monotony. The atmosphere does not change, but the viewer's relationship to it does. Expectation becomes a test rather than a forecast.

In this way, atmosphere functions as a threshold. It filters the audience before the story fully unfolds. Those willing to surrender familiar expectations find themselves aligned with the film's internal logic. Those who resist may remain outside it, observing rather than inhabiting. The film does not attempt to bridge that gap.

What remains unresolved is whether this shaping of expectation is generous or unforgiving. The atmosphere offers no apology for its severity. It insists that emotional endurance requires time, and that discomfort is not an obstacle to meaning but a condition of it. By the time the viewer realizes what the film expects of them, the question has already shifted—from what will happen next, to whether they are willing to remain within an experience that refuses to soften.

The atmosphere does not promise satisfaction. It promises immersion. Whether that immersion feels absorbing or oppressive depends entirely on the expectations the viewer is willing to let go of—and which ones they cannot.

Chapter 5 — Visual Style and World-Building

5.1 Cinematography and Lighting Choices

The cinematography of *Dracula: A Love Tale* does not seek to clarify the world so much as to limit it. Light is not treated as neutral illumination, but as an unstable condition—something that must be negotiated, rationed, and often withheld. The frame rarely feels generous. Visibility is partial, conditional, and fleeting. This is not a visual strategy designed to create suspense in the traditional sense. It creates something quieter and more corrosive: uncertainty without release.

Darkness in the film does not function as concealment. It is not there to hide sudden danger or delay revelation. Instead, it becomes the dominant state of being. Light enters the frame like memory—unreliable, selective, and never complete. Faces emerge slowly, often from one side only, as if the camera itself refuses to offer wholeness. What is revealed remains vulnerable to disappearance.

This withholding reshapes how the viewer reads emotion. Expressions are not presented cleanly. The audience must lean in, infer, accept ambiguity. Emotional clarity is never handed over. The film resists the comfort of legibility. Even moments of intimacy are framed obliquely, filtered through shadow or distance. Connection exists, but it is compromised from the outset.

Lighting sources are overwhelmingly organic: candles, fire, muted daylight filtered through stone and fabric. Artificial brightness is largely absent. This choice anchors the visual world in fragility. Flames flicker. Shadows shift unpredictably. Illumination feels temporary, even anxious. Nothing suggests permanence or control. The environment is not hostile, but it is indifferent.

This indifference matters. Horror films often weaponize darkness, using it as a threat. Here, darkness is simply the default condition. It does not act upon characters; it surrounds them. The absence of visual clarity mirrors the film's emotional logic. Certainty is not denied violently. It is denied quietly, persistently, without drama.

Camera movement reinforces this stillness. The lens rarely pursues. It observes. Shots are allowed to breathe past the point of narrative efficiency, creating a sense that time itself has slowed. When movement does occur, it feels ceremonial rather than urgent. The camera does not react; it waits. This patience creates a subtle tension, not from anticipation of action, but from the refusal to escape the moment.

The result is a visual language that discourages consumption. The film does not want to be skimmed. It demands presence. Darkness becomes an ethical choice rather than a stylistic one. To watch is to accept partial knowledge. To remain is to consent to uncertainty.

In this world, illumination never arrives as salvation. It arrives briefly, then recedes. Like love in the film, light promises intimacy but never permanence. And like love, it often reveals more than it resolves.

5.2 Production Design and Gothic Architecture

The production design of *Dracula: A Love Tale* does not seek to impress through scale alone, though scale is everywhere. Instead, it uses architecture as an emotional instrument—one that presses inward rather than opening outward. Gothic spaces dominate the film, but they are not romanticized as sites of mystery or spectacle. They are heavy. They endure. And endurance, here, is not virtuous.

Stone walls, vaulted ceilings, and vast interiors create an environment that feels less inhabited than inherited. These spaces were not built for the present moment; they were built to outlast it. Their persistence becomes oppressive. Characters move through rooms that will remain long after they are gone, and the imbalance is unmistakable. Architecture does not shelter. It reminds.

Interiors are designed to dwarf the human figure. Even when a character stands at the center of the frame, the space refuses intimacy. Ceilings rise beyond reach. Corridors stretch without promise of destination. The environment absorbs sound, motion, and presence, rendering human action small by comparison. Grandeur becomes isolation.

What is striking is the restraint of decay. The film avoids melodramatic ruin. Walls do not crumble dramatically. Structures do not collapse. Instead, erosion is slow and almost dignified. The spaces have not failed. They have simply persisted too long. This choice mirrors the film's treatment of immortality. Nothing breaks. Everything remains.

Religious architecture occupies a particularly uneasy role. Churches and sacred spaces are rendered with reverence, but never warmth. Their scale emphasizes judgment rather than comfort. Faith is present, but inaccessible. The sacred exists as an architectural fact, not a moral solution. Altars stand untouched. Symbols remain intact. Answers do not arrive.

These spaces do not invite confession or absolution. They observe. The silence within them is not peaceful; it is expectant. The architecture seems to wait, as though something unresolved has been left behind and will never be retrieved. The weight of belief lingers even when belief itself has lost its function.

Domestic spaces offer no refuge. Rooms are sparsely furnished, deliberately austere. Comfort is minimal. The absence of softness reinforces emotional severity. Nothing in these interiors encourages rest. Everything feels provisional, even when it is permanent.

The production design refuses nostalgia. The past is not presented as a place of lost beauty or romantic certainty. It is a burden carried forward intact. History does not fade into atmosphere; it presses into the present. Time accumulates rather than passes.

In this environment, movement feels constrained not by physical barriers, but by emotional gravity. The spaces seem to insist that nothing escapes consequence. Architecture becomes memory made solid. It does not forgive. It does not forget.

5.3 Costume Design and Historical Aesthetic

Costume design in *Dracula: A Love Tale* functions as an extension of emotional stasis. Clothing does not dramatize transformation. It resists it. Garments appear heavy, layered, and deliberate, as though chosen not for expression but for endurance. Fabric clings to the body with purpose. Nothing appears ornamental.

The central figure's wardrobe is especially resistant to change. Silhouettes recur across centuries with minimal variation, creating a visual impression of arrested development. Fashion evolves around him, but he remains fixed. Time alters others. He persists unchanged. This repetition is not subtle. It is insistent.

Costumes do not signal progress. They signal persistence. The body becomes a site where the past refuses to loosen its grip. Clothing feels less like self-expression and more like armor—something worn not to impress, but to survive. The weight of fabric mirrors the weight of memory.

Color choices remain restrained throughout. Dark tones dominate, absorbing light rather than reflecting it. Occasional warmth appears, but it never asserts itself long enough to suggest relief. When lighter colors enter the frame, they feel temporary, fragile, almost out of place. Beauty exists, but it is never allowed to promise resolution.

Historical specificity is present, but it is subdued. The film does not invite admiration for period accuracy. Instead, history becomes texture. The goal is not to situate the viewer comfortably in a particular era, but to blur temporal boundaries. Centuries bleed into one another. Clothing marks time without clarifying it.

Other characters reflect movement more clearly. Their costumes change. Their bodies register the passage of years. In contrast, the central figure's visual continuity becomes unsettling. Identity hardens. The self becomes a closed system. Change occurs everywhere except where it matters most.

This refusal of visual evolution reinforces the film's moral unease. The character's devotion is not romanticized through transformation. It is exposed through stagnation. Love that does not change becomes something else— something fixed, impermeable, and ultimately violent in its resistance to loss.

Costume design, then, does not decorate the narrative. It argues with it. Clothing becomes evidence. Each repeated silhouette insists on the same unanswered question: what happens to love when it is denied an ending?

The film does not answer. It allows the body to carry the question forward, century after century, dressed in the same weight, bearing the same unresolved devotion. Nothing falls away. Nothing resolves. The aesthetic remains intact, and that intactness becomes its own indictment.

Chapter 6 – Performances and Characterization

6.1 Portrayal of Dracula as Tragic Romantic Figure

The portrayal of Dracula in *Dracula: A Love Tale* rejects the familiar extremes that have long defined the character. He is neither a purely predatory force nor a romanticized antihero designed to invite easy sympathy. Instead, the film locates him in a more difficult space: that of a tragic romantic figure whose defining trait is not cruelty or seduction, but emotional fixation. What emerges is a character shaped less by what he desires than by what he refuses to relinquish.

Tragedy, in this context, is not a matter of fate imposed from outside. It is self-sustained. Dracula's suffering originates in loss, but it is prolonged by choice—by a persistent refusal to accept the limits of human experience. Love becomes the engine of his undoing not because it is intense, but because it is eternal. The film treats this eternity not as aspiration, but as deformation. Feeling does not deepen with time; it ossifies.

Unlike traditional romantic figures whose devotion ennobles them, this Dracula is diminished by his attachment. The film is careful not to frame his love as pure or selfless. It is singular, exclusive, and immovable. The beloved becomes less a person than an idea—an absence elevated to absolute meaning. This elevation strips the relationship of reciprocity. Love no longer exists between two lives moving forward together. It exists in isolation, sustained by memory alone.

This isolation defines the character's emotional posture. He does not seek connection so much as confirmation. Encounters with others feel less like relationships than interruptions. Even when intimacy appears possible, it remains haunted by comparison. The present is never allowed to exist on its own terms. It is measured constantly against an idealized past that cannot be corrected or challenged. In this sense, Dracula's romance is fundamentally closed. It admits no growth.

The film's tragedy lies in its refusal to excuse this fixation. The audience is invited to understand its origin, but not to sanctify its consequences. Violence, manipulation, and emotional domination are framed not as aberrations, but as inevitable outcomes of love denied an ending. When attachment becomes eternal, it ceases to be ethical. It no longer adapts to the other. It demands submission.

This is where the film diverges most sharply from romanticized vampire traditions. Desire is not portrayed as liberating or transformative. It is narrowing. The world contracts around the object of devotion until nothing else holds meaning. Dracula's immortality amplifies this contraction. With no deadline, no finitude to force change, obsession hardens into identity.

The character's tragedy is therefore not that he is cursed to live forever, but that he chooses not to live differently. Time offers countless opportunities for release, but release would require surrender—an acceptance that love, like life, is shaped by loss. He cannot accept this. His tragedy is not inflicted by the supernatural. It is sustained by refusal.

What makes this portrayal unsettling is its emotional plausibility. The film suggests that the impulse to preserve love beyond death is not monstrous in itself. It is recognizably human. Grief often begins as devotion. Memory often masquerades as loyalty. The difference lies in duration. What humans experience temporarily, Dracula experiences without limit. The film stretches a familiar emotional impulse until its moral contours distort.

In doing so, it forces the viewer to confront an uncomfortable possibility: that love, when stripped of time, may become indistinguishable from possession. That devotion, when denied the dignity of an ending, may demand control rather than connection. The tragedy is not that Dracula loves too deeply. It is that he loves without permission from the living world.

The film does not resolve this tension. It allows the character to remain suspended between sympathy and judgment. He is not redeemed by his suffering, nor condemned beyond understanding. He persists, carrying his love intact through centuries, and the weight of that intactness becomes unbearable.

6.2 Supporting Characters and Their Narrative Roles

The supporting characters in *Dracula: A Love Tale* do not exist to advance plot in a conventional sense. They function instead as moral and temporal counterweights—figures defined by movement, finitude, and change. Where Dracula remains fixed, they evolve. Where he repeats, they respond. Their presence exposes the cost of his permanence by contrast rather than confrontation.

These characters are not granted equal narrative authority. They orbit the central figure, entering and exiting his life without leaving lasting marks upon him. Yet they are not incidental. Each represents a possibility that Dracula refuses: acceptance, faith, mortality, or ethical restraint. Their function is not to save him, but to reveal what he is no longer capable of becoming.

Some approach him through belief. Faith appears as an offer rather than a threat—an invitation to surrender control and accept judgment. Yet faith, in the film's moral framework, requires humility. It demands recognition of limits. Dracula cannot accept this without relinquishing the identity he has built around loss. Religious figures therefore become reminders of an alternative he rejects. They are not enemies so much as witnesses.

Others approach through desire or affection, offering the possibility of connection in the present tense. These encounters are marked by imbalance. The living characters move toward him with curiosity or longing, while he measures them against an absence they cannot compete with. The asymmetry is profound. The supporting characters are capable of change. They hope, fear, and adapt. He does not. Their vulnerability exposes his rigidity.

Women in the narrative, in particular, are positioned at the intersection of devotion and erasure. They are asked to carry the weight of projection—to resemble, to echo, to substitute. Their individuality exists, but it is continually overshadowed by expectation. This dynamic is not framed as romantic destiny. It is framed as emotional violence, quiet and persistent. The film does not dramatize this violence loudly. It allows it to unfold through imbalance and silence.

Other figures embody time itself. Aging bodies, shifting loyalties, and moral hesitation remind the audience that life, when allowed to proceed naturally, is defined by impermanence. These characters experience loss and continue. They do not escape grief, but they survive it by allowing it to change them. In their presence, Dracula's refusal becomes more pronounced. He is not tragic because he has lost. He is tragic because he has not moved.

The supporting characters do not offer solutions. They do not form a collective resistance or moral judgment. Their roles are quieter. They demonstrate what it means to live within limits. They carry grief without allowing it to calcify. They accept contradiction without demanding eternity as compensation.

In many scenes, these characters appear briefly, then vanish from the narrative, leaving little trace. This ephemerality is deliberate. It reinforces the imbalance between mortal life and immortal fixation. People pass through Dracula's existence like moments through time—felt, then gone. He remains unchanged. The cost of this permanence is isolation so complete that even interaction becomes hollow.

The film resists turning these figures into instruments of redemption. No one arrives with the power to correct or save the central figure. Their failure to do so is not framed as weakness. It is framed as inevitability. Redemption, if it exists at all, cannot be imposed from outside. It would require surrender from within.

In this way, the supporting characters deepen the film's central question without answering it. They show what love looks like when it is allowed to end, to change, to be wounded and yet remain ethical. Against this backdrop, Dracula's devotion appears increasingly severe—not because it is passionate, but because it is impermeable.

What lingers is not the absence of opposition, but the absence of transformation. The supporting characters live, change, and disappear. Dracula remains. And in that remaining, the film locates its quiet indictment: that eternity, when built on refusal rather than acceptance, does not preserve love. It imprisons it.

6.3 Emotional Impact of the Performances

The emotional impact of the performances in *Dracula: A Love Tale* does not announce itself through intensity or display. It settles gradually, accumulating weight through restraint. The actors are not asked to persuade the audience of emotion so much as to endure it. Feeling is carried, not performed. What emerges is a register of acting that feels less expressive than burdensome, as though each character is moving under the pressure of something that cannot be spoken aloud.

The central performance is built almost entirely on containment. Emotion rarely breaks the surface in obvious ways. Grief does not erupt; it persists. Love is not declared; it is assumed, carried as a permanent condition rather than a momentary state. The performance relies on stillness—on the refusal to release feeling even when circumstances might demand it. This stillness is not passive. It is tense, deliberate, and exhausting to maintain.

What makes this approach emotionally affecting is its resistance to catharsis. The actor does not offer the audience relief through confession or breakdown. Pain is never externalized enough to become consumable. Instead, it remains locked within the body, visible only through small gestures: a hesitation before movement, a gaze that lingers too long, a posture that suggests vigilance rather than rest. These details do not ask for empathy directly. They allow it to form slowly, or not at all.

The performance asks the viewer to do emotional work. Sympathy is not guaranteed. At times, the character's emotional fixation feels oppressive, even alienating. Yet the actor never pushes the audience away intentionally. The emotional distance that develops feels earned, a consequence of devotion hardened into rigidity. The performance refuses to soften the character in order to be liked. It accepts discomfort as part of its emotional truth.

Supporting performances operate in a different register, one defined by movement and vulnerability. These characters are allowed a wider emotional range. They hesitate, react, hope, and doubt. Their faces register time. Their bodies age, tire, and respond. In contrast to the central figure's containment, these performances feel porous. Emotion passes through them rather than lodging permanently.

This contrast is crucial to the film's emotional architecture. The supporting actors do not compete for intensity. They reveal what change looks like. Their grief moves. Their love adapts. Their fear alters behavior. These performances ground the film in mortality, reminding the audience of emotional rhythms that include endings. Against this backdrop, the central performance becomes increasingly severe—not because it is louder, but because it does not evolve.

Interactions between characters are marked by imbalance. Conversations feel weighted toward one side, as though emotional exchange cannot fully occur. Supporting characters reach outward; the central figure remains fixed inward. This asymmetry generates unease. The audience senses emotional harm without overt conflict. The performances allow this harm to exist without naming it.

Notably, moments of tenderness are handled with particular care. They are brief, restrained, and often interrupted—not by external forces, but by emotional hesitation. Touch, when it occurs, feels tentative rather than assured. Eye contact replaces dialogue. Silence carries meaning that words would dilute. These choices prevent sentimentality. Affection is present, but it is fragile, easily overwhelmed by memory and expectation.

The emotional impact of the performances is cumulative rather than immediate. Viewers may leave individual scenes unsure of what they felt, only to realize later that something has settled heavily. The acting does not aim for memorability in isolated moments. It aims for persistence. Feeling does not peak; it remains.

What ultimately gives the performances their power is their refusal to resolve the audience's emotional response. The actors do not guide viewers toward pity, condemnation, or forgiveness. They allow contradiction to remain intact. The central figure can be understood without being absolved. Supporting characters can be empathized with without being idealized. No one is simplified for emotional clarity.

By the end of the film, the emotional residue left by these performances feels less like satisfaction than like pressure. Something has been sustained too long. Something has not been released. The acting does not offer closure; it deepens unease. Love remains heavy. Grief remains active. The audience is left not with a feeling resolved, but with one that continues to ask for attention.

In this way, the performances do not function as emotional guides. They function as emotional conditions. To watch them is not to be led, but to remain alongside—to share, however briefly, the burden of feeling that refuses to end.

Chapter 7 – Music, Sound, and Emotional Resonance

7.1 The Role of the Score in Storytelling

The score in *Dracula: A Love Tale* does not function as accompaniment. It does not arrive merely to underline emotion or signal how a scene should be felt. Instead, it behaves like an internal voice—sometimes aligned with the image, sometimes pressing against it, sometimes refusing to recede when silence might feel safer. Music becomes less a guide than a presence, shaping the emotional weather of the film with a persistence that borders on insistence.

Rather than responding to narrative beats, the score often anticipates or prolongs them. It enters scenes early, lingers after they end, and occasionally refuses to withdraw at moments when restraint might offer relief. This approach mirrors the film's central emotional condition: feeling that does not know how to stop. Just as the protagonist's love persists beyond its natural span, the music frequently sustains emotion beyond the moment that produced it.

The melodies themselves are weighted, elegiac, and repetitive. Themes recur with minimal variation, reinforcing a sense of fixation. The score does not evolve dramatically as time passes. Like the central figure, it remains anchored to a limited emotional vocabulary, returning again and again to the same motifs. What might initially feel like continuity slowly begins to feel like confinement.

This repetition is not without purpose. It reflects a world in which emotional progress has stalled. The music does not narrate transformation because transformation does not occur. Instead, it reinforces stasis. Each recurrence of a theme feels less like reminder and more like evidence—proof that nothing has shifted beneath the surface.

At its most effective, the score deepens the film's sense of tragic inevitability. It draws attention to the emotional cost of endurance, making the passage of time feel heavy rather than expansive. Music becomes a reminder that feeling, when unchanging, can become oppressive. The score does not console. It insists.

Yet this insistence also creates tension with the image. At times, the music feels almost too present, crowding moments that might otherwise breathe. This friction is not accidental, but it is risky. The score's refusal to step back can intensify immersion, but it can also limit interpretive space. When music occupies emotional territory too fully, it leaves less room for ambiguity.

The film seems aware of this risk, and yet unwilling to retreat from it. The score's dominance becomes part of the film's argument: that emotional excess, even when beautiful, can overwhelm. Music, like love, becomes something that presses inward, shaping experience through repetition rather than release.

7.2 Sound Design and Its Influence on Mood

If the score functions as emotional pressure, the sound design functions as emotional texture. It operates quietly, often unnoticed, shaping the film's atmosphere through absence as much as presence. Sound does not fill space so much as define its boundaries. Silence is not emptiness here; it is weight.

Ambient sound is restrained. Wind, footsteps, distant echoes—these elements are present, but subdued. They do not create realism so much as isolation. The world feels hushed, as though sound itself has learned to conserve energy. This restraint heightens the sense of emotional suspension. Nothing intrudes suddenly. Nothing demands attention. Everything waits.

When sound does assert itself, it often does so through repetition rather than shock. Doors open and close with deliberate heaviness. Fabric shifts audibly. Breath becomes noticeable. These details ground the film in physical presence without breaking its stillness. The body is always present, even when emotion remains withheld.

Silence plays a crucial role. Extended quiet moments allow the viewer to become aware of their own expectations. Accustomed to sound as cue, the audience begins to listen for something that never arrives. This waiting becomes part of the experience. The absence of sound mirrors the absence of resolution. The film does not rush to fill the void.

Dialogue is handled with particular restraint. Voices are rarely raised. Words are measured, often sparse. Conversations feel less like exchanges than like parallel monologues that fail to meet. This disconnection reinforces the emotional isolation at the heart of the film. Even when characters speak, something remains unsaid.

The sound design also reinforces the film's sense of time as suspended. Echoes linger longer than expected. Rooms seem to absorb sound slowly, as though unwilling to let it go. These acoustic choices create the impression that the environment itself is holding on, just as the central character does. Sound, like memory, refuses to dissipate cleanly.

Together, silence and subtle sound create an atmosphere that is neither peaceful nor tense in the conventional sense. It is anticipatory without anticipation, heavy without threat. The mood does not build toward something. It settles and remains. Sound design does not drive the narrative forward; it holds it in place.

7.3 When Music Enhances—and When It Overwhelms

The tension between enhancement and excess defines the film's relationship with music. At its best, the score deepens emotional resonance without dictating response. It amplifies feeling without clarifying it, allowing ambiguity to remain intact. In these moments, music feels like an extension of the film's inner life, inseparable from image and mood.

There are scenes where the score's persistence feels earned. Moments of loss, longing, and reflection are allowed to unfold slowly, with music reinforcing their gravity rather than rushing them toward sentiment. Here, the score does not tell the audience what to feel; it sustains the emotional field in which feeling emerges.

Yet there are also moments when the music threatens to overwhelm the image. When emotional cues are layered too heavily, the viewer's interpretive role narrows. Music begins to speak louder than gesture, louder than silence. The film risks replacing emotional complexity with emotional insistence.

This imbalance is not catastrophic, but it is revealing. It reflects the same contradiction that defines the central character. Just as devotion becomes excessive when it refuses limits, music becomes overwhelming when it refuses restraint. The film seems willing to accept this risk, perhaps even to embrace it. Excess becomes thematic rather than accidental.

What complicates this further is that the moments of overwhelm are not always distinguishable from the moments of success. What one viewer experiences as operatic intensity, another experiences as emotional saturation. The score does not adjust itself to the audience's threshold. It remains fixed, insisting on its presence regardless of reception.

This refusal to moderate reinforces the film's divisive nature. Music does not soften the experience or guide it toward consensus. It sharpens difference. Viewers are forced to confront their own tolerance for emotional density. The question becomes not whether the score is too much, but whether "too much" is precisely the point.

By allowing music to verge on excess, the film aligns sound with its broader exploration of permanence without release. The score does not resolve. It repeats. It lingers. It refuses to fade gracefully. In doing so, it mirrors the emotional state it depicts.

The final effect is unresolved. Music enhances and overwhelms in equal measure, sometimes within the same scene. The film does not correct this imbalance. It leaves it exposed. The audience is left to decide whether the score deepened the experience or crowded it—or whether that tension itself is part of what the film is trying to express.

In *Dracula: A Love Tale*, sound does not offer comfort. It offers endurance. And endurance, as the film repeatedly suggests, is not always a virtue.

Chapter 8 – Central Themes and Interpretations

8.1 Love, Loss, and Eternal Longing

Love in *Dracula: A Love Tale* is not presented as an experience that unfolds and completes itself. It is presented as a condition that arrests time. From the beginning, affection is bound to loss so tightly that the two become indistinguishable. Love does not precede loss here; it is defined by it. What the film examines is not romance as fulfillment, but longing as identity.

Loss arrives early, but it never recedes. It does not evolve into memory or soften into nostalgia. Instead, it becomes a fixed point around which everything else organizes itself. The beloved is not allowed to remain human—finite, flawed, capable of contradiction. She becomes absolute. In elevating love to this level, the film quietly removes its capacity for reciprocity. Love ceases to be an exchange. It becomes preservation.

Eternal longing, as the film imagines it, is not dramatic. It is repetitive. It returns in gestures, in silences, in the refusal to recognize the present as valid on its own terms. The central figure does not seek love again; he seeks recognition of what was. The future exists only as a space in which the past might be restored. This is not hope. It is fixation.

What makes this longing unsettling is its emotional plausibility. The impulse to hold on—to refuse the finality of loss—is deeply human. Grief often begins with loyalty. Memory can feel like devotion. The film does not condemn this impulse outright. Instead, it stretches it beyond its natural span. When longing is denied an ending, it begins to hollow out the world around it.

Love, in this framework, becomes exclusionary. Everything that does not participate in the original bond is rendered secondary. New relationships are not judged on their own merits; they are measured against an ideal that cannot respond or change. The living are forced into comparison with the dead, and they inevitably fail. The past becomes tyrannical precisely because it cannot be challenged.

The film's portrayal of eternal longing is therefore not romantic in the conventional sense. It is severe. It asks what happens when love refuses mortality. Without the pressure of time, love no longer needs to adapt. It does not negotiate difference. It does not risk vulnerability. It simply persists. And persistence, the film suggests, is not the same as devotion.

Loss is what gives love its shape. Without loss, love has no boundary. It expands until it consumes everything else. The tragedy at the center of the film is not that love survives death, but that it survives unchanged. What should have been transformed by grief instead becomes entrenched by it.

This is where the film's treatment of longing diverges from sentimentality. Longing is not framed as beautiful suffering. It is framed as emotional paralysis. Time moves forward, but the self does not. The world becomes something to be endured rather than inhabited. Eternity offers no new meaning; it only multiplies the absence that came before it.

The film does not suggest that love must end to be meaningful. It suggests that love must be allowed to change. Eternal longing denies that possibility. It freezes affection at its most intense moment and refuses the work of living that follows loss. In doing so, it transforms love into something rigid, impermeable, and ultimately destructive.

What remains unresolved is whether this longing is tragic because it is excessive, or because it is too sincere. The film does not clarify. It allows love to remain both understandable and devastating. The audience is left to sit with the possibility that the most dangerous form of devotion is not hatred or cruelty, but refusal—the refusal to let love become something else when time demands it.

8.2 Faith, Curse, and the Question of Redemption

Faith in *Dracula: A Love Tale* exists not as certainty, but as pressure. It is present everywhere—in architecture, ritual, language—yet it rarely offers solace. The sacred appears intact, but inaccessible. This distance between belief and comfort becomes central to the film's moral tension. Faith does not resolve suffering here. It witnesses it.

The curse at the heart of the story is often framed as supernatural, but its deeper form is ethical. Immortality is not punishment imposed from above; it is consequence embraced from within. The transformation that follows loss is not depicted as an act of rebellion alone, but as a refusal to submit to finitude. Faith demands acceptance of limits. The curse emerges where that acceptance breaks down.

Redemption, then, becomes a complicated proposition. Traditional narratives offer redemption as reward— something earned through suffering or repentance. This film is more ambivalent. It asks whether redemption is even possible when the self has been constructed around refusal. To be redeemed would require surrendering the very identity that immortality has preserved.

Faith offers an alternative path, but it is not an easy one. It requires relinquishing control, acknowledging that love does not grant exemption from loss, and accepting judgment without guarantee of reunion. This is a form of humility that the central figure cannot tolerate. Faith demands trust in an order beyond personal desire. Eternal longing demands the opposite.

The film does not portray faith as cruel or oppressive. It portrays it as incompatible with fixation. Religious figures and symbols do not threaten; they invite. Yet the invitation itself becomes unbearable. To accept faith would mean admitting that love does not justify eternity, that devotion does not override moral consequence. It would mean allowing the beloved to remain gone.

The curse functions as a mirror to this refusal. Immortality preserves the body, but corrodes meaning. The world continues, but without orientation. Faith, with its emphasis on endings and judgment, offers structure. The curse offers duration without direction. In choosing immortality, the character chooses continuation over coherence.

What complicates the question of redemption is that the film never fully aligns itself with faith as solution. The sacred is distant, often silent. Prayers go unanswered. Rituals feel empty. Redemption, if it exists, is not guaranteed by belief alone. The film resists turning faith into a corrective force that neatly resolves suffering.

Instead, redemption appears as a question rather than a promise. Is redemption possible without relinquishing love? Or does redemption require letting love die in its original form? The film does not resolve this tension. It allows faith to remain present but unfulfilled, offering structure without certainty.

The curse, then, is not merely vampirism. It is the preservation of self against change. Faith challenges this preservation by insisting on transformation. Redemption would require movement—away from fixation, away from possession, toward acceptance of loss as final. Whether such movement is possible after centuries of refusal remains unanswered.

What the film ultimately suggests is that redemption cannot coexist with eternal longing in its current form. Something must give. Either love must change, or immortality must end. Faith gestures toward this truth without enforcing it. The curse delays the decision indefinitely.

In leaving the question unresolved, the film refuses moral closure. It does not declare faith triumphant or longing damned. It allows both to exist in uneasy proximity. The audience is left to confront a difficult possibility: that redemption is not denied by cruelty or disbelief, but by devotion that refuses to accept an ending.

Faith waits. The curse persists. And between them remains a love that has outlived its moral shape, suspended in a time that offers no resolution—only endurance.

8.3 Immortality as Punishment Rather Than Power

Immortality in *Dracula: A Love Tale* is stripped of the allure it so often carries in myth. It is not framed as dominance over time, nor as liberation from human frailty. It is framed as consequence. The film treats eternal life not as an expansion of possibility, but as a narrowing—an existence in which choice diminishes as duration increases. What appears at first as power reveals itself, slowly and relentlessly, as punishment.

The familiar fantasy of immortality promises mastery: endless time, endless knowledge, endless opportunity. This film dismantles that promise by refusing to show immortality as growth. Time passes, but nothing accumulates in a meaningful way. Experience does not deepen into wisdom. Memory does not resolve into understanding. Instead, everything circles a single emotional axis. Eternity becomes repetition without progress.

What the film suggests is that power requires change in order to remain power. Without the pressure of endings, action loses urgency. Decision loses weight. When nothing is at stake, everything becomes arbitrary. Immortality erodes consequence not by eliminating pain, but by making pain permanent. Suffering no longer teaches; it simply persists.

This persistence reshapes the self. Identity hardens around the moment of loss that made immortality desirable in the first place. Rather than moving through grief, the immortal becomes a custodian of it. Memory ceases to be reflective and becomes prescriptive. The past dictates the present with absolute authority. In this way, immortality does not preserve the self as it was—it freezes the self at its most wounded point.

The film repeatedly resists portraying immortality as enhancement. Physical strength, heightened senses, supernatural abilities—these are present, but they feel incidental. They do not bring satisfaction or clarity. They function more like compensations than rewards, tools that enable survival without offering meaning. Power exists, but it is empty. It serves continuation, not fulfillment.

This emptiness becomes more pronounced as the mortal world continues to change. Others age, adapt, forget, and move on. They lose and recover. Their lives are shaped by rhythm: beginnings, middles, endings. The immortal stands outside this rhythm, unable to participate fully in any of it. Relationships become asymmetrical. Every connection carries an expiration date that applies only to one side. Intimacy is always provisional. Loss is guaranteed.

In this context, immortality resembles exile rather than supremacy. The immortal is not elevated above humanity; he is separated from it. He watches life proceed at a pace that no longer corresponds to his own experience. Time becomes something he inhabits without belonging to. This separation is not dramatic. It is quiet, cumulative, and deeply isolating.

The film underscores this isolation by refusing to romanticize the long view. Centuries do not grant perspective. They intensify fixation. The longer the immortal exists, the more entrenched his emotional posture becomes. There is no evidence that time itself heals. Without finitude, there is no imperative to reconcile, forgive, or transform. Immortality removes the necessity of emotional labor.

This is where punishment becomes most apparent. The immortal is not forced to suffer by an external authority. He is forced to endure himself. Eternity becomes an enclosure. The self, unchallenged by death, becomes inescapable. There is no reset, no release, no forgetting. Identity becomes static, and stasis becomes torment.

Power, traditionally, implies agency. It implies the ability to alter one's condition or environment in meaningful ways. The immortality depicted here undermines agency by removing the conditions that make choice matter. When there is always more time, there is no urgency to change. When consequences can be deferred indefinitely, responsibility loses force. The immortal's greatest power—endurance—becomes his greatest limitation.

The film also suggests that immortality corrupts moral judgment. Without the prospect of an ending, ethical boundaries blur. Actions lose proportionality. Harm becomes easier to justify when time stretches endlessly forward. Violence can be rationalized as temporary.

Exploitation can be framed as necessity. The immortal's moral compass, no longer calibrated by mortality, drifts.

This drift is not portrayed as villainy. It is portrayed as erosion. The film does not accuse the immortal of choosing evil. It shows how immortality gradually dismantles the structures that make ethical choice coherent. Without death, there is no final accounting. Without finality, there is no reckoning. Punishment becomes internal rather than imposed.

The absence of death also alters the meaning of survival. Survival ceases to be achievement and becomes obligation. The immortal does not live because he chooses to, but because he cannot stop. Existence becomes compulsory. The film frames this compulsion as one of the most severe consequences of immortality. To live forever is to lose the right to decide when life has run its course.

In moments where the immortal appears powerful—commanding space, exerting control, outlasting others—the film subtly undercuts the spectacle. These moments are never framed as triumphs. They feel hollow, almost mechanical. Power without purpose reveals itself as burden. Control without endpoint becomes monotony.

The punishment of immortality is not immediate. It unfolds slowly, almost imperceptibly. At first, endurance feels like resistance. Later, it feels like inertia. Eventually, it feels like entrapment. The film allows this progression to remain largely unspoken, trusting the accumulation of time and repetition to convey its weight.

What makes this portrayal particularly unsettling is its inversion of desire. Immortality is initially sought as escape from loss. Over time, it becomes the very mechanism by which loss is perpetuated. The beloved does not return. The wound does not close. Instead, the immortal is condemned to carry absence intact across centuries. Eternity does not undo death. It magnifies it.

The film resists offering immortality as a moral lesson in the conventional sense. It does not declare that eternal life is wrong or unnatural. It simply observes what happens when life is stripped of its ending. Meaning thins. Attachment hardens. Power loses direction. Punishment emerges not as pain inflicted, but as life prolonged beyond its capacity to transform.

By framing immortality this way, the film challenges a deep cultural fantasy. It suggests that what humans fear most—death—is also what allows love, choice, and morality to remain alive. Without death, love cannot change. Without endings, identity cannot loosen its grip. Immortality preserves the self at the cost of becoming human.

The film leaves the viewer with an unresolved tension. If immortality is punishment, what does that imply about the desire to escape death? Is the wish itself misguided, or is the tragedy that it is granted at all? The film does not answer. It allows the question to linger, heavy and uncomfortable.

In the end, immortality is not depicted as power lost or power abused. It is depicted as power misunderstood. What appears limitless is, in fact, confining. What promises freedom delivers fixation. Eternity does not elevate the immortal above humanity. It isolates him from the very conditions that give life its meaning.

And so immortality endures in the film not as triumph, but as sentence—one that contains no clear parole, only the endless continuation of a self that can no longer change, waiting in a time that no longer moves toward anything at all.

Chapter 9 — Narrative Strengths and Achievements

9.1 Emotional Ambition and Romantic Scope

The emotional ambition of *Dracula: A Love Tale* is neither modest nor cautious. It does not aim to persuade through charm or efficiency. It aims to overwhelm through duration. The film's romance is not expansive in the sense of breadth, but in its refusal to contract. Love is allowed to occupy the entire emotional field, crowding out all other impulses until it becomes indistinguishable from identity itself.

This ambition is risky. Romantic narratives often rely on modulation—on moments of relief, humor, or contrast that allow feeling to circulate rather than stagnate. This film refuses modulation. It commits fully to intensity and holds that commitment without apology. Love does not rise and fall; it persists. The scope of the romance is therefore not measured by how much it includes, but by how little it allows to exist outside it.

What the film attempts is not to make love appealing, but to make it absolute. Devotion is not one emotional strand among many; it is the organizing principle of the world. All other relationships feel provisional. All other values feel secondary. The romance does not coexist with life—it replaces it. In doing so, the film tests the limits of audience endurance as much as it tests the moral limits of devotion itself.

This scale of emotional ambition is rare in contemporary cinema, not because filmmakers lack interest in love, but because few are willing to explore its darker implications without retreating into irony or restraint. *Dracula: A Love Tale* does neither. It insists that love, when stretched beyond mortality, becomes something that no longer resembles the comfort it promises. The film does not soften this transformation. It watches it unfold.

The romantic scope is also temporal. Centuries pass, yet the emotional premise remains unchanged. This refusal to let love evolve becomes the film's central provocation. Is love still love if it cannot adapt? Is devotion virtuous if it demands permanence? The film does not answer these questions. It allows them to expand until they fill the narrative space entirely.

The ambition lies not in resolving these tensions, but in sustaining them. The film dares to believe that emotional excess can carry meaning without collapse. Whether it succeeds for every viewer is beside the point. What matters is that it attempts something few films are willing to sustain for this long: romance without relief.

9.2 Visual Grandeur and Artistic Confidence

The film's visual grandeur is inseparable from its confidence. *Dracula: A Love Tale* does not hedge its aesthetic choices. It commits to scale, darkness, and severity with a steadiness that suggests neither insecurity nor apology. Grandeur here is not decorative; it is structural. The film believes in its images enough to let them linger, even when they risk alienation.

What distinguishes this grandeur from spectacle is its restraint. The film does not chase visual excess through constant motion or overwhelming detail. Instead, it allows scale to assert itself through stillness. Vast spaces are held in frame long enough to become oppressive. Architecture dwarfs the human figure not to impress, but to diminish. Beauty is present, but it is heavy.

This confidence extends to the film's willingness to repeat itself visually. Motifs recur. Compositions echo one another across time. Rather than signaling creative exhaustion, this repetition reinforces the film's thematic core. The visual world does not evolve because the emotional world does not. The film trusts that the audience will recognize this parallel without being instructed.

Artistic confidence also appears in the film's refusal to clarify meaning through emphasis. Images are not underlined. Symbols are not isolated. The camera does not direct attention aggressively. Instead, it allows viewers to sit with ambiguity, to notice patterns gradually or not at all. This trust in the audience is itself a form of confidence.

There is a risk inherent in this approach. Grandeur without variation can become monotony. Stillness can drift into inertia. The film seems aware of this risk and accepts it. It does not adjust its visual language to accommodate restlessness. It maintains its severity even when that severity becomes uncomfortable. In doing so, it asserts that discomfort is not failure, but part of the experience it offers.

The result is a film that feels authored rather than assembled. Each visual decision appears to emerge from a coherent internal logic rather than from external expectation. Whether one finds the result absorbing or excessive, the confidence behind it is unmistakable. The film knows what it wants to be, and it does not dilute itself to be more easily received.

9.3 Moments Where the Film Truly Succeeds

The film's most successful moments are rarely its loudest or most elaborate. They occur in stillness, in hesitation, in the spaces where nothing resolves. These moments succeed not because they provide clarity, but because they sustain tension without collapse. They trust silence. They trust duration. They trust the audience to remain present without reward.

One such success lies in the film's treatment of intimacy. When characters draw close, the camera does not rush to sanctify the moment. Touch is tentative. Proximity feels dangerous rather than reassuring. The absence of emotional release in these scenes reinforces the film's central idea: that closeness, when shaped by fixation, can become oppressive rather than comforting.

Another success emerges in the film's handling of time. Transitions between eras do not announce themselves dramatically. They slide into one another, blurring historical boundaries. This subtlety reinforces the sense that time has lost its authority. The audience experiences temporal disorientation not as confusion, but as condition. The film succeeds here by aligning form with meaning.

The performances also contribute to these moments of success, particularly in scenes where emotion is implied rather than stated. A look held too long. A silence allowed to stretch. A gesture that does not complete itself. These choices create emotional resonance without instruction. The film trusts understatement to carry weight.

Perhaps the film's most significant success lies in its refusal to offer moral resolution. It does not guide the audience toward forgiveness or condemnation. It allows sympathy and discomfort to coexist. The absence of closure feels deliberate rather than evasive. The film succeeds by leaving its central questions intact, resisting the impulse to tidy them into lesson or warning.

There are moments when the film's ambition strains its execution, when repetition threatens to dull rather than deepen. Yet even these moments feel consistent with the work's internal logic. Excess is not an accident here; it is a risk the film knowingly takes. In accepting that risk, the film preserves its integrity.

Ultimately, the film succeeds not by satisfying expectation, but by maintaining coherence. Its emotional, visual, and thematic elements remain aligned even when they become difficult to endure. The work does not fracture under the weight of its own seriousness. It holds.

What lingers after the film is not a single image or scene, but a sustained emotional pressure. Something has been carried too long. Something has not been allowed to end. The film succeeds in making the audience feel that weight— not briefly, but persistently.

And in that persistence, uncomfortable and unresolved, the film finds its quiet strength.

Chapter 10 — Critical Challenges and Divided Opinions

10.1 Pacing, Excess, and Narrative Restraint

Pacing in *Dracula: A Love Tale* is not a neutral technical choice. It is an ethical one. The film does not move slowly by accident, nor does it do so out of indulgence alone. Its slowness is bound to its central refusal: the refusal to let emotion resolve, the refusal to allow time to heal what it normally erodes. The narrative advances, but it does so reluctantly, as though movement itself were a betrayal of the emotional condition it seeks to inhabit.

This restraint places the film in a precarious position. It asks the audience to remain within a single emotional register for an extended duration, without the relief of contrast or escalation. Scenes often arrive already heavy and leave without lightening. There is little modulation, little sense of narrative breathing room. What might, in another film, be trimmed or displaced is allowed to remain. Silence stretches. Repetition accumulates. Time presses inward rather than outward.

Excess emerges not through spectacle, but through duration. The film's most controversial indulgence is its willingness to stay too long in moments that conventional storytelling would abandon sooner. This staying is deliberate. It mirrors the central figure's inability to move on. The audience is not merely observing stasis; it is asked to experience it. The pacing enforces empathy through endurance rather than identification.

Yet this approach carries risk. Excess of duration can erode tension as easily as it can deepen it. When scenes linger without clear transformation, the line between contemplation and inertia becomes fragile. For some viewers, the film's restraint registers as discipline—a refusal to simplify or rush emotional truth. For others, it feels like a failure of narrative economy, an insistence that mistakes persistence for profundity.

The film appears aware of this tension and unwilling to resolve it. It does not attempt to correct its own excesses through late-stage acceleration or explanatory payoff. Instead, it commits to a form of narrative restraint that is almost austere in its severity. The story withholds information not to create mystery, but to preserve ambiguity. Motivation is implied rather than clarified. Consequence is suggested rather than dramatized.

What complicates the critique of pacing is that the film's excess is not evenly distributed. Some sequences feel essential in their slowness, allowing emotional weight to surface gradually. Others test patience without offering new insight, repeating affect without deepening it. The film does not distinguish clearly between these moments, leaving the audience to decide whether repetition is thematic or merely cumulative.

Narrative restraint, in this context, becomes a refusal to editorialize. The film does not step in to reassure the viewer that their patience will be rewarded. It does not signal which moments matter more than others. This lack of hierarchy can feel either liberating or punishing. The viewer must do the work of discernment without guidance.

What emerges is a film that treats restraint not as minimalism, but as pressure. By denying conventional pacing cues, it creates a sustained emotional compression. Time does not pass cleanly. Scenes do not resolve decisively. The audience remains inside a narrative that feels resistant to progress. This resistance is thematically coherent, but coherence does not guarantee comfort.

The question, then, is not whether the film is too slow or too excessive, but whether its pacing aligns with its moral ambition. The film seems to argue that emotional fixation cannot be depicted efficiently without betrayal. To compress the story would be to deny its subject. Whether that argument convinces depends on the viewer's tolerance for endurance as meaning.

10.2 Story Choices That Polarize Viewers

The polarization surrounding *Dracula: A Love Tale* is not incidental. It arises directly from the film's most fundamental story choices—choices that refuse compromise, clarity, or consensus. The film does not hedge its emotional or moral positions. It commits to ambiguity and accepts division as consequence.

One of the most polarizing choices is the film's refusal to frame its central figure as either villain or victim. The narrative offers access to his grief without granting absolution for his actions. It invites understanding without endorsement. This moral ambiguity unsettles viewers accustomed to clearer ethical signposts. Sympathy becomes uncomfortable. Judgment feels insufficient. The film does not intervene to stabilize this tension.

Another divisive choice lies in the film's treatment of romance. Love is not softened or idealized. It is portrayed as consuming, exclusionary, and ultimately destructive when denied finitude. For some viewers, this feels like a necessary corrective to romantic mythology. For others, it feels punitive or bleak, stripping romance of its aspirational dimension. The film does not attempt to reconcile these readings. It allows romance to remain morally compromised.

The narrative's resistance to resolution further deepens polarization. Key emotional and thematic questions are left open, sometimes uncomfortably so. The film does not provide a definitive moral stance on devotion, immortality, or redemption. Viewers seeking clarity may experience this as evasive or incomplete. Others may see it as intellectually honest, an acknowledgment that such questions cannot be neatly answered.

Temporal structure also contributes to division. The film's fluid handling of time—its blurring of eras, its resistance to clear progression—can feel immersive or disorienting. Some viewers experience this as poetic, reinforcing the sense of eternal stasis. Others find it alienating, a barrier to emotional engagement. The story does not orient itself around historical markers; it orients itself around feeling. That choice privileges atmosphere over comprehension.

Even the film's moments of beauty can polarize. Visual grandeur, when sustained without contrast, risks being read as indulgent. The film's commitment to darkness, stillness, and repetition can feel operatic to some, oppressive to others. The narrative does not modulate its aesthetic to accommodate differing thresholds. It assumes a willingness to remain within severity.

Perhaps most divisive is the film's apparent indifference to being liked. It does not court the audience through charm or reassurance. It does not offer humor, irony, or relief as points of entry. This seriousness can feel refreshing to viewers hungry for uncompromising cinema. It can also feel exclusionary to those who expect engagement to include accessibility.

What unites these polarizing choices is their consistency. The film does not contradict itself in an attempt to satisfy multiple audiences. It remains aligned with its central vision even when that vision limits its reach. The resulting division feels less like failure than like consequence.

Polarization, in this case, becomes a measure of the film's integrity. The story refuses to smooth its contradictions for the sake of coherence or approval. It allows discomfort to persist, trusting that meaning can emerge from sustained tension rather than resolution.

The film does not ask to be agreed with. It asks to be endured, considered, and argued over. In doing so, it accepts that some viewers will turn away. Others will remain. The story choices that divide are the same ones that define it.

What remains unresolved is whether division itself is a virtue. The film offers no defense beyond its own existence. It presents its choices fully formed and steps back. The audience responds not with consensus, but with fracture.

And in that fracture, the film finds its final provocation: not whether it succeeded, but whether success was ever its goal.

10.3 Why the Film Has Sparked Debate

The debate surrounding *Dracula: A Love Tale* did not arise from misunderstanding alone. It emerged because the film occupies a space that contemporary cinema often avoids: the space where emotional seriousness is not softened by irony, where moral complexity is not resolved into reassurance, and where ambition is allowed to exceed comfort. The film does not merely invite disagreement; it structures itself around conditions that make agreement unlikely.

At the center of this debate is the film's refusal to clarify its own moral stance. Viewers are accustomed to narratives that signal where sympathy should rest and where judgment should fall. Even films that claim ambiguity often guide the audience subtly toward resolution. This film withholds that guidance. It presents actions and consequences without editorial correction. Love causes harm. Grief justifies cruelty. Devotion erases others. These realities are shown, not explained away. The audience is left to sit with them without instruction.

For some, this refusal feels honest. It respects the complexity of human emotion and the impossibility of clean moral accounting. For others, it feels evasive, as though the film is avoiding responsibility by declining to take a position. The debate forms precisely here: is moral ambiguity a form of rigor, or a failure of conviction?

The film's treatment of romance intensifies this tension. Romance is often granted moral immunity in storytelling.

Passion excuses transgression. Devotion redeems violence. *Dracula: A Love Tale* strips romance of that immunity. Love is not presented as inherently virtuous. It is shown to be capable of exclusion, domination, and erasure when it refuses limits. This challenges deeply held cultural assumptions about love as an unquestioned good.

For viewers invested in romantic mythology, this portrayal can feel like an attack. The film does not merely complicate romance; it subjects it to ethical scrutiny. It asks whether devotion remains noble when it denies autonomy to others, when it demands permanence at any cost. These questions provoke discomfort because they extend beyond the film. They touch personal beliefs about love, loyalty, and loss.

Debate also emerges from the film's stance toward suffering. Suffering is not framed as purifying or ennobling. Endurance does not lead to insight. Pain does not produce growth. The central figure suffers endlessly and remains unchanged. This challenges a narrative expectation deeply embedded in storytelling: that suffering must justify itself through transformation. Here, suffering simply persists.

Some viewers interpret this as bleakness, even nihilism. Others see it as a refusal to lie about the limits of endurance. The film does not promise that pain makes us better. It suggests that pain, when preserved without interruption, may make us rigid. This suggestion unsettles because it undermines a comforting moral economy.

The film's pacing further fuels debate by forcing viewers to experience this endurance rather than merely observe it.

Slowness becomes participatory. The audience is asked to share, however briefly, the sensation of emotional stasis. This demand can feel profound or punishing. It exposes differing expectations about what cinema owes its audience. Is film obligated to reward patience? Or is the experience itself the point?

Debate intensifies when this pacing intersects with expectations of genre. Horror audiences may feel deprived of catharsis. Romance audiences may feel deprived of hope. Art-house audiences may feel challenged, but not necessarily satisfied. The film does not align itself cleanly with any one set of expectations, and this misalignment produces friction.

Another source of contention lies in representation and agency. The film's handling of supporting characters— particularly women—has provoked scrutiny. They are often positioned as reflections, echoes, or vessels for the central figure's fixation. Their inner lives are present but constrained by the narrative's focus. Some viewers interpret this as critique: a deliberate exposure of how obsession erases individuality. Others interpret it as repetition of the very dynamic it depicts.

The debate here hinges on intent versus effect. Does the film successfully interrogate emotional domination, or does it reproduce it without sufficient resistance? The film does not resolve this question. It does not provide counterweights strong enough to neutralize discomfort. As a result, viewers must decide whether the unease they feel is purposeful or problematic.

Faith and redemption introduce further complexity. The film gestures toward spiritual frameworks without embracing them as solutions. Faith is present, but distant. Redemption is possible, but undefined. This ambiguity frustrates viewers who expect metaphysical clarity. Others find value in the refusal to simplify belief into answer. The debate reflects broader cultural uncertainty about faith's role in meaning-making.

What distinguishes this debate from routine polarization is its persistence. Responses to the film rarely settle quickly. Viewers continue to argue, reconsider, and reframe their interpretations over time. The film does not exhaust itself on first viewing. Its questions linger, and with them, disagreement.

This persistence suggests that the debate is not merely about taste, but about thresholds—thresholds for emotional density, moral uncertainty, and aesthetic severity. The film exposes these thresholds by refusing to adjust itself to meet them. It remains constant. Viewers change in response.

The debate is also fueled by the film's seriousness. In an era saturated with self-aware storytelling and tonal hybridity, *Dracula: A Love Tale* offers no escape hatch. It does not wink at the audience. It does not soften its implications with humor or detachment. This earnestness can feel refreshing or exhausting. It demands to be taken seriously, and that demand itself provokes resistance.

Ultimately, the film has sparked debate because it resists consensus at every level. It does not clarify its morality, soften its romance, accelerate its pacing, or stabilize its genre identity. It refuses to negotiate. In doing so, it forces viewers to confront not only the film's ideas, but their own expectations about art, love, and endurance.

The debate does not end with agreement because the film does not aim for agreement. It aims for confrontation—quiet, sustained, and unresolved. The discomfort it generates is not a side effect. It is the mechanism by which the film continues to live beyond the screen.

What remains after the arguments fade is not a verdict, but a question that refuses to settle: whether a film that divides so deeply has failed its audience, or whether it has asked more of them than they were prepared to give.

Chapter 11 —
Representation and
Modern Sensibilities

11.1 Female Characters and Narrative Agency

The female characters in *Dracula: A Love Tale* exist within a narrative gravity that consistently pulls them toward the central figure's emotional orbit. Their presence is significant, often luminous, yet rarely autonomous. Agency, in this film, is not denied outright; it is constrained, shaped, and redirected by a story that privileges endurance of devotion over the freedom of becoming.

Women appear as figures of meaning before they are allowed to be figures of choice. They are loved intensely, remembered obsessively, sought across time—but this intensity does not translate into narrative authority. Instead, it renders them symbolic. They become anchors for memory, vessels for projection, and sites upon which longing is inscribed. Their inner lives exist, but they are frequently subordinated to what they represent rather than who they are.

This dynamic is not subtle. The film repeatedly positions female characters as the emotional justification for action rather than as agents of action themselves. Their desires are acknowledged, yet they rarely alter the trajectory of the story. Even when they resist, that resistance is absorbed into the central figure's narrative rather than allowed to redirect it. Choice becomes momentary; consequence remains elsewhere.

What complicates this portrayal is the film's apparent awareness of the imbalance it depicts. The erasure of agency is not romanticized through triumph or fulfillment. It is rendered as quiet harm. The women are not portrayed as fulfilled by their symbolic roles. They experience confusion, fear, hesitation, and loss of selfhood. The film allows these effects to surface, but it does not always allow them to challenge the structure that produces them.

This raises an unresolved tension between depiction and critique. On one level, the film exposes how obsessive devotion can erase individuality, particularly when one person's memory dominates another's present. On another level, it risks reproducing that erasure by failing to grant female characters sufficient narrative space to exist beyond the central fixation. The line between examination and repetition remains deliberately unstable.

Female characters are often positioned at moments of decision that never quite become theirs. They are asked to resemble, to echo, to carry forward something that predates them. Identity is shaped by expectation rather than discovery. The weight of the past presses down upon them, leaving little room for self-definition. In this sense, the film's treatment of women mirrors its treatment of time: both are constrained by what refuses to end.

The emotional cost of this dynamic is evident. The women in the film are not passive in temperament, but they are rendered passive by narrative design. Their suffering does not lead to transformation or empowerment. It accumulates quietly. The absence of release becomes part of the film's larger pattern of endurance without resolution.

The discomfort this generates is not accidental. The film seems willing to let the audience sit with the implications of emotional domination rather than correct them. Yet it stops short of offering a counter-narrative strong enough to rebalance agency. As a result, viewers are left to decide whether the film is critiquing the reduction of women to symbols, or whether it is trapped within the very structure it portrays.

This ambiguity fuels debate because it refuses moral clarity. The film does not present female agency as something reclaimed or restored. It presents its absence as a condition—one produced by obsession, sustained by immortality, and left unresolved. The women endure. The story moves on. And what lingers is the question of whether endurance alone is being mistaken for significance.

11.2 Gothic Tradition Versus Contemporary Values

Dracula: A Love Tale draws heavily from gothic tradition, yet it does so without fully reconciling that tradition with contemporary ethical expectations. Gothic narratives have long been fascinated with excess—excess of emotion, excess of devotion, excess of suffering. They operate in heightened moral landscapes where obsession is romantic, sacrifice is noble, and endurance is proof of depth. The film inherits these impulses intact.

Within gothic tradition, women often function as symbols before they function as subjects. They represent purity, temptation, loss, or redemption. Their value lies in what they signify rather than what they choose. *Dracula: A Love Tale* embraces this lineage openly. It does not attempt to modernize the gothic by softening its hierarchies. Instead, it presents them with a seriousness that borders on severity.

This choice creates friction with contemporary values that emphasize autonomy, consent, and interior complexity. Modern audiences are attuned to the ethical implications of stories where devotion overrides agency. The film does not adjust its gothic inheritance to align comfortably with these values. It allows the tension to remain visible.

In doing so, the film occupies an uneasy position. It neither fully critiques the gothic framework nor fully endorses it. The story unfolds according to gothic logic—where love justifies obsession and memory overrides present reality—yet it unfolds in a cultural context increasingly skeptical of those assumptions. The result is a work that feels out of time, not in setting, but in moral orientation.

This dissonance is central to the film's impact. Gothic tradition thrives on imbalance: power disparities, emotional extremes, moral ambiguity. Contemporary values seek balance, voice, and accountability. The film stages a collision between these impulses without offering synthesis. It does not resolve gothic excess into modern critique. It allows them to coexist uncomfortably.

Some viewers interpret this as deliberate confrontation. The film becomes a space where outdated romantic ideals are exposed through their consequences. Obsession appears suffocating rather than seductive. Eternal devotion appears imprisoning rather than noble. From this perspective, the film uses gothic tradition to reveal its own ethical limits.

Others interpret the same elements as failure to evolve. By leaning so heavily into gothic tropes without sufficiently reframing them, the film risks reinscribing the very values it might be interrogating. The lack of explicit critique becomes troubling in a contemporary context that expects narratives to acknowledge power imbalances rather than simply depict them.

What complicates the debate is the film's refusal to mediate between past and present. It does not translate gothic language into modern reassurance. It allows the old forms to speak in their own voice, severe and uncompromising. This refusal can feel artistically honest or ethically negligent, depending on the viewer's threshold for ambiguity.

The gothic has always been a genre of excess and transgression. Its power lies in its willingness to dwell in moral darkness without illumination. *Dracula: A Love Tale* honors that lineage. Whether it should have interrogated it more forcefully is an open question—one the film declines to answer.

By placing gothic tradition intact within a contemporary frame, the film creates a productive unease. It forces viewers to confront how much of the romantic mythology they are willing to accept without revision. The discomfort does not resolve into lesson or condemnation. It lingers.

In that lingering tension between inherited form and present values, the film locates one of its most challenging questions: whether some myths are meant to be corrected, or whether their power lies precisely in their refusal to adapt.

11.3 Cultural and Ethical Questions Raised

The cultural and ethical questions raised by *Dracula: A Love Tale* do not emerge as arguments. They emerge as pressures. The film does not pose its concerns in the language of critique or commentary; it embeds them within emotional experience and allows their implications to unfold slowly. What lingers is not a message, but an unease that resists resolution.

At the center of this unease is the question of how culture understands devotion. The film challenges the assumption—

deeply rooted in romantic tradition—that love justifies endurance at any cost. Devotion, here, is not framed as mutual or sustaining. It is singular, isolating, and possessive. The beloved becomes an object of permanence rather than a participant in change. This raises an uncomfortable ethical question: when does loyalty become refusal, and when does memory become domination?

Culturally, the film unsettles the idea that intensity is proof of sincerity. Modern narratives often equate emotional extremity with authenticity. The more one suffers, the more one must love. *Dracula: A Love Tale* resists this equation. It suggests that intensity, when left unchecked, may hollow out moral responsibility rather than affirm it. Love that does not adapt becomes exclusionary. It demands continuity rather than consent.

The film also interrogates the cultural valorization of endurance. Endurance is often celebrated as virtue—an indication of strength, loyalty, or resilience. In this story, endurance is ambiguous. The central figure survives everything, yet nothing improves. He persists, but he does not heal. This persistence raises a difficult question: is endurance meaningful when it preserves harm as faithfully as it preserves love?

Ethically, the film complicates the notion of agency within asymmetrical relationships. Immortality creates an imbalance that cannot be neutralized by affection. One party exists beyond time; the other does not. Consent, choice, and reciprocity become fragile under such conditions. The film does not dramatize this imbalance through overt coercion. It allows it to exist quietly, normalized by devotion. This quiet normalization is precisely what makes it troubling.

The cultural weight of myth further complicates these dynamics. Dracula is not merely a character; he is a symbol shaped by centuries of retelling. Each iteration carries inherited assumptions about masculinity, power, and desire. *Dracula: A Love Tale* does not discard these assumptions. It presents them intact, forcing viewers to confront what they still carry. The ethical discomfort arises not from novelty, but from recognition.

The film also raises questions about how culture treats grief. Grief is often framed as something to be overcome, transformed into wisdom or acceptance. Here, grief is allowed to remain unresolved. It becomes identity rather than passage. The ethical tension lies in whether grief, when preserved indefinitely, ceases to honor the lost and begins to erase the living. The film does not moralize this shift. It allows its consequences to accumulate.

Another question emerges around responsibility across time. Immortality disrupts conventional moral accounting. Actions lose proportion when consequences stretch endlessly forward. The film asks whether moral responsibility requires finitude in order to remain meaningful. Without an endpoint, can accountability still function? Or does it dissolve into justification and delay?

Culturally, the film unsettles the fantasy of transcendence. Immortality is often imagined as escape—from death, from limitation, from consequence. This story reframes transcendence as detachment. To live forever is to lose alignment with the rhythms that give life ethical shape. The film suggests that mortality is not merely a biological fact, but a moral one. It anchors responsibility, urgency, and care.

The ethical questions raised by the film are not abstract. They intersect with contemporary conversations about power, autonomy, and emotional entitlement. The central figure's devotion mirrors cultural narratives that excuse control in the name of love, persistence in the name of loyalty, and harm in the name of memory. The film does not condemn these narratives directly. It allows them to unfold to their logical end.

What makes these questions difficult is that the film offers no corrective framework. Faith is distant. Redemption is uncertain. Love does not redeem itself. There is no external authority that steps in to restore balance. The ethical landscape remains unsettled, forcing the viewer to confront the discomfort without guidance.

This refusal to resolve ethical tension is itself a cultural statement. It resists the expectation that stories must instruct as well as depict. Instead, the film trusts the audience to sit with ambiguity, to recognize the cost of unresolved devotion without being told what to conclude.

In the end, the cultural and ethical questions raised by *Dracula: A Love Tale* are not questions the film answers.

They are questions it refuses to quiet. They remain active, pressing against inherited myths and modern values alike, asking whether some forms of love are dangerous not because they are cruel, but because they refuse to end.

The film does not offer reassurance that these questions can be settled. It leaves them suspended, much like the figure at its center—enduring, unresolved, and ethically unstable.

Chapter 12 — Comparison with Other Dracula Adaptations

12.1 Classic Interpretations of Dracula

Classic interpretations of Dracula have tended to stabilize the myth by fixing its moral coordinates. Whether framed as monstrous invader, aristocratic predator, or seductive embodiment of forbidden desire, Dracula traditionally exists in opposition to the living world. He threatens social order, moral clarity, and bodily autonomy. The narrative tension arises from this threat and resolves through confrontation, containment, or destruction.

In early literary and cinematic forms, Dracula functions as an external force. His power lies in intrusion. He crosses borders—geographical, sexual, spiritual—and destabilizes those he encounters. The horror emerges from violation rather than intimacy. Fear is produced through difference. Dracula is terrifying because he is other.

Even when later interpretations soften the figure, granting him interiority or tragic backstory, the underlying structure remains intact. Sympathy is permitted, but it rarely displaces judgment. Love may motivate Dracula, but it does not redefine him. He is still framed as a problem to be solved, a curse to be lifted, or a force to be neutralized. The narrative ultimately restores balance by reaffirming mortality, morality, and human continuity.

Romanticized versions often lean into seduction, turning Dracula into an object of fascination rather than pure dread. Yet even here, desire is usually framed as dangerous but temporary. The story warns rather than lingers. Romance intensifies the threat but does not replace it. The vampire's allure is meant to be resisted, not endured.

Across these classic interpretations, time functions as a stabilizing force. The story moves forward. The vampire appears, disrupts, and is confronted. Even when the ending is tragic, it is final. The myth resets itself through resolution. Dracula's power lies in disruption, but his meaning is contained by closure.

What unites these interpretations is a shared confidence in narrative authority. The story knows where it stands. It knows who is wronged, who is threatened, and what must be done. Ambiguity exists, but it is managed. The myth survives by repeating a structure that reassures even as it frightens.

12.2 How *Dracula: A Love Tale* Breaks from Tradition

Dracula: A Love Tale breaks from this tradition not by rejecting the myth's elements, but by rearranging their moral weight. The film removes the familiar anchor of opposition. Dracula is no longer positioned primarily against society, faith, or the living. He is positioned against time. The conflict is not externalized through pursuit or invasion. It is internalized through fixation.

This shift alters the story's entire orientation. The vampire is not a disruption that arrives and must be expelled. He is a condition that persists. The narrative does not build toward confrontation; it circles around endurance. The absence of a clear antagonist dissolves the familiar rhythm of threat and response. What remains is stasis.

Romance, rather than intensifying danger, becomes the film's central structure. Love is not a temptation to be resisted or a weakness to be exploited. It is the organizing principle of existence. This devotion does not redeem the character; it isolates him. By allowing love to dominate the narrative completely, the film removes the possibility of balance. There is no counterforce strong enough to restore proportion.

The film also breaks from tradition by refusing to restore moral clarity. It does not frame Dracula's actions as justified, but it does not frame them as aberrations either. They emerge logically from emotional fixation. The audience is not invited to cheer his downfall or fear his survival. Judgment becomes unstable.

Time, in this version, does not resolve conflict. It magnifies it. Centuries pass without transformation. This is a radical departure from traditional structures where time leads toward resolution. Here, time erodes meaning rather than producing it. The film denies the myth its usual narrative release.

Even genre boundaries are unsettled. Horror recedes. Romance deepens. Gothic atmosphere remains, but it no longer promises confrontation or catharsis. The film does not reject tradition outright; it allows tradition to exhaust itself. By lingering where other versions would move on, it exposes the limits of inherited forms.

12.3 What This Version Adds to the Myth

What *Dracula: A Love Tale* adds to the myth is not a new origin or a revised set of rules, but a sustained interrogation of permanence. The film extends a question that earlier interpretations gesture toward but rarely inhabit: what happens when love is denied the dignity of an ending?

By centering the myth on emotional endurance rather than predation, the film reframes Dracula as a study in fixation rather than power. Immortality becomes a mechanism for preserving grief intact. Love becomes an argument against change. This shift adds a new moral dimension to the myth, one that does not rely on fear or temptation to generate unease.

The film also contributes a deeper ambiguity around redemption. Traditional versions often align redemption with death, destruction, or sacrifice. This version withholds that clarity. Redemption, if it exists at all, remains undefined. The myth is allowed to remain morally unresolved. This refusal becomes part of its meaning.

Perhaps most significantly, the film adds duration as a form of critique. By forcing the audience to experience emotional stasis rather than merely observe it, the story transforms endurance into a burden rather than a virtue. The myth is no longer about what Dracula does, but about what he cannot stop doing.

This version also exposes the ethical cost of romantic absolutism. By allowing love to eclipse agency, reciprocity, and consent, the film reveals how easily devotion can slide into domination. This is not presented as lesson or warning, but as consequence. The myth gains a new capacity to unsettle contemporary assumptions about love's moral immunity.

What the film adds is therefore not comfort or clarity, but pressure. It presses the myth against modern sensibilities without resolving the friction. It allows the story to remain unresolved, heavy, and ethically unstable.

In doing so, *Dracula: A Love Tale* does not replace earlier interpretations. It complicates them. It adds a layer of introspection that refuses closure. The myth survives once again—not by repeating itself, but by asking what it means to endure when nothing is allowed to end.

Chapter 13 — Cultural and Cinematic Context

13.1 Gothic Romance in Contemporary Film

Gothic romance has never disappeared from cinema, but its function has changed. In earlier eras, the genre thrived on heightened emotion and moral excess, offering audiences a space where desire and danger intertwined without apology. In contemporary film, however, gothic romance exists in tension with an audience trained to expect irony, psychological realism, and ethical clarity. Its language is older than the cultural moment it now inhabits, and that dissonance shapes how it is received.

Modern gothic romance no longer assumes shared belief in fate, eternal devotion, or moral absolution. Instead, it operates as a pressure test. It asks whether these ideas can still be sustained without collapsing under scrutiny. Many contemporary films soften the genre by reframing it as fantasy, nostalgia, or metaphor—ways of enjoying excess without fully endorsing it. Others fracture it through self-awareness, allowing audiences to keep emotional distance.

Dracula: A Love Tale resists both strategies. It does not apologize for its seriousness, nor does it dilute gothic romance into aesthetic shorthand. It treats the genre not as an inherited style, but as a living emotional structure—one capable of producing discomfort when taken at face value. Love is excessive. Devotion is absolute. Time is irrelevant. These are not decorative qualities; they are demands.

In contemporary cinema, where emotional restraint is often equated with maturity, such intensity can feel regressive or provocative. Gothic romance insists that feeling does not need to be moderated to be meaningful. It also insists that excess has consequences. By allowing romance to dominate rather than complement the narrative, the film exposes how gothic ideals strain under modern ethical awareness.

This places *Dracula: A Love Tale* at odds with a cinematic landscape that prefers balance. The film does not integrate gothic romance into a broader tonal palette. It commits to it fully. That commitment makes the genre visible again—not as style, but as moral force. The film asks whether gothic romance can still function honestly in a world less willing to accept devotion without question.

13.2 Why This Story Resonates Today

The resonance of *Dracula: A Love Tale* lies not in novelty, but in recognition. The film speaks to a contemporary anxiety about permanence in a culture defined by instability. In an era of rapid change—technological, social, emotional— the idea of something enduring, unchanging, and absolute carries both appeal and threat. The film does not offer permanence as comfort. It offers it as burden.

Modern audiences are increasingly aware of the costs of emotional absolutism. Narratives that once celebrated unwavering devotion now invite skepticism. The film's portrayal of love that refuses to adapt mirrors real-world conversations about boundaries, autonomy, and emotional entitlement. Devotion that eclipses the self of another no longer reads as noble by default. It reads as dangerous.

At the same time, the film taps into a widespread exhaustion with disposability. Relationships, identities, and values often feel provisional. The desire for something that lasts—for love that does not erode under pressure—remains powerful. *Dracula: A Love Tale* occupies the uneasy space between these impulses. It acknowledges the longing for permanence while refusing to romanticize its consequences.

The story also resonates because it treats grief as unresolved rather than transformative. Contemporary culture often frames healing as progress: loss must lead to growth, insight, or closure. This film resists that narrative. Grief persists. It shapes identity. It does not guarantee wisdom. This portrayal aligns with lived experience more closely than with cultural expectation, and that alignment can feel both validating and unsettling.

The figure of Dracula, reimagined as emotionally fixed rather than monstrously aggressive, becomes a metaphor for what happens when mourning is denied an endpoint. In a world increasingly attentive to mental health, trauma, and emotional labor, this metaphor lands with particular force. The film does not offer recovery. It offers recognition.

What resonates, ultimately, is the film's refusal to reassure. It reflects a moment in which certainty feels dishonest and resolution feels premature. By leaving its central questions open, the story mirrors a cultural landscape where answers are provisional and ethics remain contested.

13.3 Audience Reception Across Different Markets

Audience reception of *Dracula: A Love Tale* has varied significantly across markets, shaped as much by cultural context as by cinematic expectation. The film's seriousness, pacing, and emotional density are not universally legible in the same way. Responses reveal less about the film's coherence than about the assumptions audiences bring with them.

In European markets, particularly those with strong traditions of art-house cinema, the film has often been approached as a character study rather than a genre piece. Viewers familiar with slower pacing and moral ambiguity tend to engage with the film on its own terms. The emphasis on atmosphere, endurance, and unresolved tension aligns with cinematic traditions that value interiority over momentum. Debate exists, but it often centers on interpretation rather than legitimacy.

In contrast, audiences in markets more accustomed to genre-driven storytelling—where horror and romance follow clearer structural rhythms—have responded with greater polarization. Some viewers feel misled by expectations attached to the Dracula name. The absence of catharsis, escalation, or clear moral framing registers as denial rather than intention. Others respond positively to this deviation, welcoming a version of the myth that refuses spectacle.

Streaming-era viewing habits also shape reception. The film's demand for sustained attention conflicts with modes of consumption built around interruption and multitasking. Viewers encountering the film outside a theatrical context may experience its pacing as heavier, its repetition more pronounced. In this sense, reception is shaped not only by culture, but by medium.

Critical response across markets reflects similar divides. Praise often focuses on ambition, coherence, and emotional seriousness. Criticism tends to emphasize excess, narrative inertia, and ethical discomfort. What is consistent is the absence of indifference. The film provokes response even when it alienates.

These variations underscore the film's resistance to universality. *Dracula: A Love Tale* does not adapt itself to regional expectations. It travels intact, allowing each market to respond according to its own thresholds for ambiguity and endurance. Meaning shifts not because the film changes, but because context does.

What emerges from this uneven reception is a portrait of a film that functions less as entertainment product than as cultural object. It absorbs projection, resistance, and debate differently depending on where it lands. The fractures in response are not flaws to be corrected. They are evidence of the film's unwillingness to neutralize itself for global consensus.

In crossing borders without smoothing its edges, the film reveals something essential about contemporary audiences: not that they disagree about quality, but that they disagree about what cinema should ask of them.

Chapter 14 – SPOILERS: Breakdown of the Final Act

14.1 Events Leading to the Climax

The movement toward the climax in *Dracula: A Love Tale* does not follow the familiar arc of escalation. There is no sudden acceleration, no sharp pivot into action that signals arrival. Instead, the film approaches its final movement the same way it has approached everything else—through accumulation. What leads to the climax is not a chain of events so much as the gradual exhaustion of possibility.

By this point in the film, repetition has taken on a new weight. Encounters echo earlier encounters. Conversations feel like variations rather than developments. The past presses closer, no longer content to remain background. What once felt like endurance begins to feel like inevitability. The narrative tightens not by adding stakes, but by removing alternatives. Options narrow quietly.

The emotional atmosphere grows denser rather than louder. Silence carries more force. Glances linger with greater consequence. The world does not change, but the cost of remaining unchanged becomes harder to ignore. The film's central tension—between devotion and release, between endurance and surrender—no longer feels theoretical. It has become unbearable.

What distinguishes this approach is the absence of narrative urgency as signal. The film does not announce that it is approaching a decisive moment. There is no musical cue or visual rupture that declares transition. The sense of culmination arises internally, through a growing awareness that the conditions sustaining the story cannot continue indefinitely without collapse.

The beloved figure—whether present physically or through memory—exerts increasing pressure. The past is no longer something remembered; it is something reenacted. This reenactment does not promise restoration. It exposes distortion. What once felt pure now feels rigid. What once justified endurance now demands reckoning.

The mortal world, too, asserts itself more forcefully in this final stretch. Time becomes visible again—not as abstraction, but as loss. Bodies age. Loyalties shift. Faith wavers. These reminders do not interrupt the central figure's fixation; they surround it, tightening the emotional space until there is nowhere left to retreat.

The events leading to the climax therefore feel less like steps forward than like a closing circle. The film returns to its origin point—loss—but now stripped of illusion. The endurance that once felt defiant begins to feel compulsory. Immortality no longer reads as resistance; it reads as entrapment.

By refusing spectacle, the film makes the approach to climax feel intimate and severe. The audience is not swept toward a conclusion. It is pressed toward one. The question is no longer what will happen, but whether anything can still change without breaking the emotional logic the film has sustained.

14.2 Key Decisions and Turning Points

The key decisions in *Dracula: A Love Tale* are not framed as moments of dramatic choice. They arrive quietly, often without clear articulation. This subtlety is deliberate. The film resists the idea that transformation announces itself cleanly. Change, when it comes at all, emerges through hesitation rather than declaration.

The central turning point is not an act of violence or sacrifice, but a confrontation with limit. For the first time, endurance itself is questioned—not externally, but from within. The figure who has survived centuries without altering course is forced to reckon with the possibility that continuation is no longer neutral. To persist is no longer merely to exist; it is to choose harm knowingly.

This realization does not produce immediate action. The film refuses the comfort of decisive clarity. Instead, it lingers in the moment where choice becomes unavoidable but remains unmade. The weight of centuries presses against the present, and for the first time, the pressure is felt as moral rather than emotional.

Other turning points occur through absence rather than intervention. Faith does not arrive to redeem. Love does not return to justify endurance. The world does not offer a corrective force strong enough to restore balance. These absences function as decisions imposed by reality. They strip away illusion by refusing to cooperate with desire.

Supporting characters play a crucial role here, not by persuading or confronting, but by withdrawing. Their inability—or refusal—to remain within the central figure's emotional orbit creates a rupture. Isolation, once chosen, becomes enforced. The cost of fixation is no longer theoretical. It is lived.

One of the film's most significant decisions is its refusal to dramatize these turning points as triumph or defeat. There is no clear victory in letting go, nor clear damnation in continuing. The film understands that either path carries loss. Release means surrendering identity. Endurance means perpetuating harm. The narrative does not privilege one outcome over the other.

This ethical stalemate is the film's true climax. Action, when it occurs, feels almost secondary to recognition. The most consequential shift is internal: the acknowledgment that love, as it has been preserved, cannot coexist indefinitely with responsibility. Whether this acknowledgment leads to transformation or merely deepens tragedy is left deliberately uncertain.

By handling its turning points with restraint, the film preserves the ambiguity it has cultivated from the beginning. Decisions do not resolve tension; they expose it. The climax does not answer the film's central questions. It sharpens them.

What lingers after these moments is not closure, but consequence. Something irreversible has been recognized, even if it has not been undone. The story does not end with certainty, but with awareness—and with the uneasy knowledge that awareness alone may not be enough to save anyone involved.

14.3 Immediate Consequences of the Final Scenes

The immediate consequences of the final scenes in *Dracula: A Love Tale* are not delivered as resolution, but as aftermath. The film does not close its narrative by restoring order or clarifying meaning. Instead, it leaves behind a changed emotional landscape—one marked less by action completed than by recognition endured. What follows the climax is not release, but residue.

The most striking consequence is the collapse of illusion. Whatever belief sustained the central figure—whether faith in reunion, justification through devotion, or the neutrality of endurance—can no longer be held without fracture. The final scenes strip these beliefs of their protective ambiguity. Love, preserved without alteration, is revealed not as salvation but as confinement. This revelation does not correct the past; it exposes it.

Yet exposure does not equal transformation. The film is careful here. It does not suggest that recognition automatically leads to change. The consequences are psychological before they are narrative. A threshold has been crossed internally, but the external world remains largely the same. Time continues. The immortal condition persists. What has altered is the moral weight of continuation. To go on is no longer innocent.

For the central figure, the immediate consequence is isolation sharpened into clarity. Where solitude once felt chosen, even dignified, it now feels enforced. The emotional structures that allowed him to remain suspended—memory, repetition, ritual—no longer offer shelter. They remain, but they no longer protect. The past still dominates, but its authority is no longer unquestioned.

The living characters, where present, register a different kind of consequence. Their withdrawal is not dramatic. It does not feel like punishment or triumph. It feels like necessity. Survival requires distance. Their absence reinforces the asymmetry that has always defined the story: the immortal remains, the mortal world moves on. What changes is that this movement now feels final, not provisional.

The film does not linger on fallout in the conventional sense. There is no accounting of damage, no catalog of loss. Instead, consequence is conveyed through tone. Silence deepens. Space widens. The emotional temperature drops, not into calm, but into severity. What once felt heavy now feels exposed.

One of the most unsettling aspects of the ending is its refusal to dramatize punishment. There is no spectacle of downfall, no overt moral reckoning. The film suggests that punishment has already been in effect all along. Immortality itself remains the sentence. What changes is the awareness of that sentence. To recognize one's imprisonment without escape is its own form of consequence.

This restraint resists audience expectation. Viewers accustomed to narrative justice may search for balance— some confirmation that harm has been answered. The film offers none. It does not validate the desire for moral symmetry. Instead, it presents a world where consequence is uneven, prolonged, and unresolved.

The final scenes also recalibrate the meaning of endurance. What once appeared as defiance now reads as inertia. Survival no longer carries dignity. It feels compulsory. The immortal does not stand triumphant at the end. He remains. And remaining, after everything has been exposed, feels heavier than before.

What lingers most immediately is the sense that nothing has been fixed, yet nothing can return to what it was. The emotional ground has shifted, even if the physical circumstances have not. The film closes not with conclusion, but with an altered condition—one in which love has been stripped of its moral alibi, and immortality has been stripped of its illusion of power.

The consequence, then, is not an ending, but a narrowing. Possibility has not expanded; it has contracted. The future feels less open, not more. The story does not promise that awareness will lead to redemption. It suggests only that ignorance is no longer possible.

In this way, the final scenes do not resolve the film's central tensions. They leave them intact, but heavier. What the audience is left with is not closure, but a sustained ethical pressure—the knowledge that something essential has been recognized too late, and that recognition alone may not be enough to undo the cost of having endured without change for so long.

Chapter 15 – The Ending Explained

15.1 Interpreting the Film's Conclusion

The conclusion of *Dracula: A Love Tale* resists interpretation in the way it resists everything else: by refusing to stabilize. It does not offer a symbolic key that unlocks meaning, nor does it guide the viewer toward a single emotional or moral outcome. Instead, it closes by narrowing the field of possibility until interpretation itself becomes the final act required of the audience.

What the ending makes clear is not what has changed, but what cannot be undone. The film does not resolve its central tension between endurance and release; it exposes that tension as permanent. Any hope that the story might pivot toward redemption, punishment, or reconciliation is quietly withdrawn. The conclusion denies the satisfaction of transformation while insisting on the reality of consequence.

One way to read the ending is as an ethical arrest. The central figure reaches a point where continuation can no longer be mistaken for neutrality. To go on is no longer simply to exist, but to affirm a pattern of harm already understood. The film does not show whether this recognition alters behavior. It shows only that ignorance has ended. In this reading, the conclusion is not an ending at all, but a beginning stripped of innocence.

Another interpretation reads the ending as tragic stasis rather than moral awakening. Recognition arrives too late to matter. The self has been shaped too completely by fixation to permit change. Awareness becomes another burden rather than a catalyst. The film allows this interpretation to stand alongside the first, refusing to privilege growth over entrapment.

What the conclusion refuses most forcefully is narrative compensation. There is no sense that suffering has earned wisdom, or that love has justified endurance. The story does not close with equilibrium restored or imbalance corrected. Instead, it leaves the central figure exactly where he has always been—enduring—but now without illusion. The endurance remains, but its meaning has shifted from defiance to exposure.

The ambiguity of the conclusion is not evasive. It is precise. The film understands that any definitive statement about meaning would contradict its core argument: that some emotional states cannot be resolved without falsifying them. By withholding closure, the film preserves the integrity of its central condition. The ending does not solve the story. It crystallizes it.

To interpret the conclusion, then, is not to decode it, but to decide what weight recognition carries when it arrives without escape. Is awareness itself a form of change? Or does it merely sharpen the pain of permanence? The film offers no answer. It allows interpretation to remain unstable, mirroring the unresolved endurance it depicts.

15.2 Love, Death, and Redemption

Love, death, and redemption form the film's final constellation, but they do not align into harmony. They remain in tension, each undermining the promises of the others. Love does not conquer death. Death does not grant release. Redemption does not arrive to reconcile what has been preserved too long.

The film's treatment of love at its conclusion is unsentimental. Love is neither condemned nor celebrated. It is revealed. What remains is not affection in motion, but devotion arrested at the moment of loss. This love does not grow, forgive, or adapt. It endures unchanged, and that endurance is shown to be its most troubling feature. Love survives death, but in doing so, it forfeits its capacity to remain ethical.

Death, traditionally the great equalizer, loses its authority here. It no longer functions as boundary or resolution. The film suggests that death gives life its moral shape precisely because it ends it. Without death, love has no limit. Without limit, love becomes absolute. And absolutes, the film insists, are where harm begins.

Redemption, if it exists at all, remains undefined. The film resists presenting redemption as reward for suffering or recognition. There is no evidence that awareness alone redeems. There is no assurance that release, if chosen, would restore balance. Redemption is not framed as something earned through endurance, nor as something guaranteed by sacrifice. It is left as a question rather than a destination.

What complicates this further is that the film does not fully align redemption with death either. Ending existence does not automatically resolve the ethical damage caused by endless devotion. The film refuses to simplify redemption into erasure. Ending suffering does not undo harm. Ending life does not retroactively justify it.

Instead, redemption hovers as an unresolved possibility that demands transformation rather than endurance. But transformation requires letting love change—and the film suggests that this is the one act the central figure has never been willing to perform. Redemption, then, is not withheld by cruelty or punishment. It is withheld by refusal.

The final impression left by the film is not despair, but severity. Love is powerful, but not sovereign. Death is final, but not redemptive on its own. Redemption is possible, but not inevitable. Each concept is stripped of its romantic certainty and left morally exposed.

In refusing to reconcile these forces, the film leaves the audience with a difficult recognition: that love does not absolve us from the need to change, that endurance is not inherently virtuous, and that redemption cannot be claimed simply by suffering long enough.

The story ends without peace, but not without clarity. What has been preserved is not innocence, but responsibility. The film closes by insisting that love, death, and redemption only retain meaning when they are allowed to transform one another. When they do not—when love refuses death, and death refuses release—what remains is not eternity, but a life prolonged beyond its moral shape.

And in that unresolved space, the film allows its final question to stand, unanswered and unsoftened: whether love that refuses to end can ever truly be redeemed, or whether redemption itself requires the courage to let love die into something else.

15.3 Multiple Readings of the Final Moments

The final moments of *Dracula: A Love Tale* do not arrive as conclusion so much as suspension. They resist being sealed into meaning, and it is precisely this resistance that allows multiple readings to coexist without collapsing into contradiction. The film does not resolve its ending because resolution would betray the emotional logic it has sustained from the beginning. What remains instead is an ending that behaves like a mirror, reflecting back the assumptions, desires, and ethical thresholds of the viewer.

One reading understands the final moments as the first genuine rupture in an otherwise unbroken endurance. From this perspective, what matters is not action but awareness. The central figure's recognition—however quiet, however incomplete—marks a departure from ignorance. The illusion that love alone justifies continuation has fractured. Even if no external change follows, something essential has shifted internally. The self can no longer pretend neutrality. The ending, then, becomes an ethical awakening delayed by centuries, fragile and uncertain, but real.

This reading does not claim redemption. It claims possibility. Awareness is not equated with salvation, only with responsibility. The final moments suggest that while the past cannot be undone, the future may no longer be inhabited blindly. The endurance that once felt inevitable now feels chosen, and choice reintroduces moral weight. In this interpretation, the ending is not hopeful, but it is no longer static. It is the moment where stasis becomes conscious.

Another reading is more severe. It interprets the final moments as confirmation that recognition arrives too late to matter. Awareness does not loosen fixation; it merely sharpens its cruelty. The self has been shaped so completely by repetition that even understanding cannot alter behavior. In this view, the ending does not mark the beginning of change, but the final enclosure of tragedy. The central figure sees clearly for the first time—and remains incapable of doing otherwise.

Here, the film's refusal of resolution becomes an indictment rather than an opening. Consciousness does not liberate; it condemns. To understand one's imprisonment without possessing the means to escape it is a deeper form of punishment. The ending, read this way, denies the audience the comfort of growth. It suggests that some patterns, once sustained long enough, cannot be broken, only recognized.

A third reading approaches the final moments not through the lens of the central figure, but through absence. What defines the ending is not what remains, but what has withdrawn. The living world recedes. Possibility narrows. Relationships dissolve not through conflict, but through necessity. In this interpretation, the ending is not about internal change at all, but about the consequences of emotional domination finally reaching their limit. The world refuses to participate any longer.

This reading emphasizes that the film's final movement belongs less to the immortal than to the mortal. The withdrawal of others becomes the decisive act. It is not redemption or damnation that defines the ending, but abandonment—not as punishment, but as survival. The immortal remains unchanged because change was never the story's only concern. The story is also about the cost borne by those who refuse to endure endlessly. The ending honors their exit without dramatizing it.

Another interpretation reads the final moments symbolically rather than psychologically. The ending becomes an articulation of the myth itself rather than the character within it. Dracula does not change because the myth does not allow change. He exists to endure. The film's refusal to resolve the ending acknowledges this structural truth. Any transformation would collapse the myth's function. The ending, therefore, is not tragic or hopeful, but faithful—to the logic of a figure defined by persistence.

In this reading, the film's conclusion is an act of restraint. It refuses to modernize the myth through therapeutic resolution. It accepts that some figures are meant to remain unresolved, carrying contradiction forward rather than overcoming it. The ending preserves Dracula as symbol rather than subject. He remains the embodiment of love that refuses finitude, and the film declines to redeem or destroy him because either act would simplify what he represents.

There is also a reading that locates the ending's meaning not in the character or the myth, but in the audience's endurance. The final moments ask whether the viewer has changed by remaining with the story this long. The film does not deliver meaning; it tests capacity. If the viewer feels unsettled, fatigued, or morally strained, that reaction becomes part of the ending. The film concludes by transferring its unresolved tension outward.

From this perspective, the multiple readings are not flaws, but mechanisms. The ending does not belong to the screen alone. It extends into interpretation, debate, and lingering discomfort. The refusal to clarify becomes an ethical gesture. The film does not resolve what it has made the audience feel; it leaves them responsible for carrying it.

These readings do not cancel one another. They overlap, contradict, and coexist. The ending supports them all because it is constructed to resist hierarchy. No single interpretation is confirmed as correct. The film does not reward decisiveness. It rewards attention.

What unites these interpretations is the recognition that the ending refuses consolation. Whether read as awakening, entrapment, withdrawal, mythic fidelity, or experiential test, the final moments deny closure. They leave the central tension intact: love preserved beyond death, endurance without transformation, awareness without escape.

The film does not ask which reading is right. It asks why the need for a single reading feels so urgent. In withholding resolution, it exposes the audience's desire for moral settlement—for reassurance that meaning can be fixed, suffering justified, devotion redeemed.

Instead, the film leaves its final moments open, heavy, and unclaimed. Meaning does not land. It lingers. The story ends not with an answer, but with an unresolved ethical pressure that continues beyond the frame, insisting that some forms of love, once extended too far, cannot be neatly interpreted—only endured, questioned, and carried forward without certainty.

Chapter 16 — Symbolism and Hidden Meaning

16.1 Recurring Visual Motifs

The visual motifs in *Dracula: A Love Tale* do not function as symbols to be decoded once and set aside. They recur with a quiet insistence, returning in altered contexts and emotional registers, accumulating meaning through repetition rather than explanation. The film trusts that significance will emerge through endurance, not emphasis. What matters is not what these motifs represent in isolation, but how they persist.

One of the most prominent motifs is stillness. Bodies pause. Frames linger. Movement, when it occurs, feels hesitant rather than decisive. This stillness is not emptiness; it is saturation. The film repeatedly places characters in states of waiting—at thresholds, in corridors, before altars, beside windows. These moments do not advance the narrative, but they deepen the condition in which the narrative exists. Waiting becomes a visual shorthand for emotional suspension, for a life held in abeyance.

Mirrors and reflective surfaces appear throughout the film, but rarely in overtly dramatic ways. They do not announce themes of duality or vanity. Instead, they offer partial reflections—distorted, dim, or fleeting. Faces appear and disappear within them, never fully captured. The motif resists self-knowledge as clarity. Reflection does not produce understanding; it produces fragmentation. Identity remains incomplete, split between memory and presence.

Another recurring motif is enclosure. Characters are frequently framed within frames—doorways, arches, windows, narrow passages. Even in vast spaces, the camera finds ways to impose containment. The world appears large, but access within it feels limited. These visual constraints reinforce the film's preoccupation with endurance without freedom. Space exists, but it does not liberate.

Hands recur with notable frequency, often isolated from the body. They reach, hesitate, withdraw. Touch is suggested more often than it is completed. When hands meet, the contact feels tentative, burdened by history. This emphasis on gesture over action underscores the film's resistance to resolution. Desire is present, but fulfillment remains elusive. The body remembers what the mind cannot release.

Blood, traditionally central to Dracula mythology, appears sparingly and without spectacle. When it does appear, it is subdued, almost ritualistic. The film avoids fetishizing it. Blood becomes less a marker of horror than of consequence. Its presence does not excite; it confirms. It reminds the viewer that harm, however restrained, remains harm.

Light itself becomes a motif through its scarcity and fragility. Candles flicker, daylight struggles to penetrate stone, shadows reclaim space quickly. Illumination never stabilizes. This instability reinforces the film's moral atmosphere. Understanding arrives briefly, then recedes. Nothing remains fully visible for long.

What unites these motifs is their refusal to culminate. They do not build toward a visual thesis. They repeat, shift slightly, and return. Meaning gathers through duration. The film does not reward attentive viewing with clarity; it rewards it with pressure. The motifs do not resolve the story's questions. They carry them forward, intact.

16.2 Religious and Mythological Symbolism

Religious and mythological symbolism in *Dracula: A Love Tale* operates without hierarchy. Sacred imagery is present, but it does not dominate or instruct. Mythological echoes surface, but they do not consolidate into allegory. The film treats belief systems not as frameworks for meaning, but as residues—structures that remain even when their authority has thinned.

Christian symbolism appears frequently, yet it is marked by distance. Crosses, altars, churches, and ritual gestures are visible, but they do not intervene. Faith exists as architecture rather than assurance. Sacred spaces are rendered with reverence, but they do not offer sanctuary. The divine is implied, never confirmed. Prayer does not produce response. The silence that follows is not dramatic; it is habitual.

This distance reframes religion as witness rather than solution. Faith observes suffering but does not correct it. Judgment is deferred indefinitely. The film does not depict religion as false, but as insufficient to contain the emotional excess it confronts. Belief remains intact, yet its capacity to restore order feels exhausted.

The curse at the center of the story carries mythological weight without clear origin. It is not explained through folklore or divine punishment. Its ambiguity allows it to function symbolically rather than narratively. Immortality becomes less a supernatural condition than a metaphysical refusal. The curse is not imposed; it is sustained. Myth here is not origin story, but ongoing state.

The film's Dracula aligns less with folkloric monster traditions than with tragic mythic figures—those who defy natural limits not out of ambition, but out of grief. Like figures condemned to endless repetition, he exists in a closed loop. His punishment is not suffering inflicted anew, but suffering preserved. Mythological time replaces historical time. Progress dissolves into recurrence.

The tension between sacred and profane remains unresolved. Sacred symbols do not dispel darkness. Profane acts do not collapse into chaos. The film resists the binary logic that often governs religious myth. Instead, it presents a world where the sacred has lost its power to resolve, and the profane has lost its power to shock. Everything exists in a state of moral fatigue.

What makes this symbolism particularly unsettling is its restraint. The film does not dramatize blasphemy or sacrilege. It allows religious imagery to coexist with transgression without spectacle. The absence of confrontation suggests that the conflict between faith and fixation has already been decided—not through triumph, but through attrition.

Mythology, in this context, becomes a language of endurance. The story does not use myth to elevate the narrative into abstraction. It uses myth to explain why abstraction fails. Immortality, curse, and sacred symbols persist because they are no longer challenged. They remain, emptied of corrective force.

The film does not reject religious or mythological frameworks. It places them in suspension, alongside love and endurance. None are granted authority over the others. Redemption is possible, but undefined. Judgment is present, but delayed. Meaning is available, but unstable.

In this symbolic landscape, belief does not redeem and myth does not resolve. They endure, much like the central figure himself—present, weighty, and unresolved. The film allows these symbols to remain intact but unfulfilled, insisting that their power lies not in what they promise, but in what they fail to deliver.

What emerges is not a critique of faith or myth, but a portrait of their limits. In a world governed by refusal to end, even the oldest stories lose their capacity to conclude. The sacred waits. The curse persists. And meaning, like redemption, remains suspended—visible, invoked, but never fully reached.

16.3 Thematic Closure and Emotional Resolution

The question of closure in *Dracula: A Love Tale* is deliberately unsettled. The film gestures toward an ending without granting one, allowing its themes to converge without resolving into harmony. What it offers instead is a form of thematic containment rather than completion—a sense that the emotional and philosophical questions it has raised have reached their fullest articulation, even if they remain unanswered.

The film achieves thematic closure not by tying its ideas together neatly, but by exhausting them. Love, loss, faith, immortality, and devotion are carried to their furthest sustainable limits. By the final movement, nothing new is being introduced; what remains is the accumulated weight of what has already been endured. The story stops not because it has finished explaining itself, but because it can no longer intensify without breaking its own logic.

Emotionally, this creates a form of resolution that feels severe rather than satisfying. The film does not aim to comfort the audience with reconciliation or release. It aims to leave them with a clarified understanding of the cost of emotional permanence. The central feeling at the end is not catharsis, but recognition. Something has been seen clearly, even if it cannot be changed.

This distinction matters. Emotional resolution is often mistaken for relief, but the film insists on a different definition. Resolution here means the stripping away of illusion. The romance has been tested and found wanting—not because it lacked sincerity, but because it refused transformation. Immortality has been revealed not as power, but as confinement. Faith has been shown to persist without intervening. These themes do not resolve into answers; they resolve into exposure.

The film's emotional closure operates through narrowing rather than expansion. Early in the narrative, possibilities feel theoretically infinite: eternal life, eternal love, endless time. By the end, those infinities have contracted. What once seemed boundless now feels claustrophobic. The emotional world has not grown richer; it has become more precise. This precision is the film's form of resolution.

Importantly, the film does not equate emotional clarity with moral correction. Awareness does not redeem. Recognition does not heal. The ending refuses the comforting belief that understanding alone is enough. Emotional insight arrives stripped of promise. It sharpens pain rather than dissolving it. This refusal is central to the film's integrity. To grant relief would be to contradict the endurance it has so carefully sustained.

Thematic closure is also achieved through consistency. By the final scenes, the film has not contradicted itself. Its treatment of love as fixation, endurance as burden, and immortality as punishment remains intact. Nothing is retroactively softened. The ending does not reinterpret earlier moments as misunderstood steps toward redemption. It confirms that what the audience has witnessed is exactly what it appeared to be.

This consistency produces a quiet finality. The story ends not because something decisive has happened, but because nothing else can. The emotional condition the film depicts has reached a point of saturation. Further continuation would not deepen understanding; it would only repeat it. In this sense, the film ends at the moment where repetition has fully revealed itself as stasis.

For the audience, this can feel like deprivation. There is no emotional release proportional to the investment required. But this deprivation is purposeful. The film suggests that some emotional states—particularly those defined by refusal—do not end cleanly. To offer resolution would be to falsify them. The lack of emotional payoff becomes a statement rather than a shortcoming.

What lingers after the film is not despair, but a disciplined severity. The viewer is left with a sharpened sense of the film's moral landscape. Love without limits corrodes. Endurance without change imprisons. Faith without surrender cannot redeem. These are not conclusions delivered as lessons; they are conditions made visible through time and repetition.

Thematic closure, then, is achieved through alignment rather than conclusion. The film's ideas, emotions, and aesthetic choices converge into a single, unrelieved state.

Nothing contradicts. Nothing resolves. The ending does not answer the film's central questions, but it confirms that those questions have been fully asked.

In refusing emotional resolution as comfort, *Dracula: A Love Tale* offers something rarer and more difficult: coherence without consolation. The story ends not by lifting its weight, but by allowing that weight to be fully felt—unredeemed, unsoftened, and intact.

Chapter 17 — Who This Film Is For

17.1 Viewers Who Will Appreciate This Interpretation

This interpretation of *Dracula: A Love Tale* will resonate most strongly with viewers who approach cinema as an experience of endurance rather than gratification. Those drawn to films that privilege atmosphere over incident, moral ambiguity over resolution, and emotional pressure over catharsis are likely to find the work compelling. The film rewards patience, not through revelation, but through coherence. It offers the satisfaction of alignment—of form, theme, and tone held together without compromise.

Viewers accustomed to art-house traditions that value interiority and restraint may recognize the film's seriousness as an invitation rather than an obstacle. The narrative's refusal to simplify love or soften consequence will feel less like denial and more like integrity. For these viewers, the absence of clear answers is not a failure of storytelling, but a recognition that some questions lose their force when resolved too cleanly.

Those interested in reinterpretations of myth that do not aim to modernize through accessibility, but through pressure, may also respond favorably. The film does not translate Dracula into contemporary comfort; it places the myth under sustained ethical strain. Viewers willing to sit with discomfort—particularly around devotion, agency, and endurance—will find that the film's severity opens space for reflection rather than closure.

This interpretation also speaks to audiences who value emotional seriousness without irony. The film's earnestness, its refusal to undercut itself with humor or detachment, will feel refreshing to viewers fatigued by tonal hybridity. It assumes attention. It does not negotiate for it.

17.2 Viewers Who May Be Disappointed

Viewers who approach the film expecting narrative propulsion, genre fulfillment, or emotional release may find the experience frustrating. The film does not accelerate toward spectacle, nor does it reward investment with resolution proportional to effort. Those accustomed to Dracula as a figure of menace, seduction, or theatrical horror may feel deprived of the pleasures traditionally associated with the myth.

Romance-oriented viewers seeking affirmation may also feel unsettled. Love here is not aspirational. It is interrogated, constrained, and ultimately revealed as ethically unstable when denied finitude. The film does not protect romance from scrutiny. For viewers who equate emotional intensity with virtue, this scrutiny can feel punitive or bleak.

The film's pacing will likely alienate audiences who rely on momentum as a marker of meaning. Scenes linger. Silence persists. Repetition accumulates without clear transformation. Viewers who interpret slowness as indulgence rather than intention may disengage before the film's internal logic fully asserts itself.

There is also the question of moral clarity. The film does not instruct. It does not frame its central figure as redeemed or condemned. Viewers who expect cinema to take a clear ethical position may experience this ambiguity as evasion. The discomfort is not alleviated. It is sustained.

17.3 Setting Expectations Before Watching

To approach *Dracula: A Love Tale* productively requires a recalibration of expectation. This is not a film that unfolds through event-driven escalation or resolves through decisive action. It is a film that accumulates. Meaning emerges through repetition, duration, and restraint. The experience is closer to inhabiting an emotional condition than following a story.

Viewers may benefit from approaching the film without genre guarantees. Horror is present, but subdued. Romance is central, but compromised. The film does not promise fear or comfort. It promises immersion. Entering with an expectation of ambiguity rather than payoff allows the film's internal coherence to become legible.

It is also useful to expect seriousness without relief. The film does not provide tonal escape hatches. There is little humor, little irony, and little modulation. This severity is not accidental. It is the means by which the film explores endurance as theme. Accepting this severity early allows resistance to soften into attention.

Finally, viewers should expect unresolved questions. The film does not aim to satisfy curiosity so much as to sharpen it. Its ending does not explain what has been endured; it confirms that endurance itself has meaning, even when that meaning is uncomfortable.

Setting expectations, then, is not about preparing for disappointment or appreciation. It is about consent. The film asks the viewer to remain—to watch without assurance of relief, to consider without promise of conclusion. Those willing to grant that consent may find the experience demanding, but coherent. Those unwilling may find it withholding.

The film does not adjust itself to the audience. It waits to see who will adjust to it.

Chapter 18 — Final Verdict

18.1 Does *Dracula: A Love Tale* **Succeed as a Gothic Reimagining?**

Whether *Dracula: A Love Tale* succeeds as a gothic reimagining depends largely on how one defines success within the gothic tradition itself. If success is measured by fidelity to atmosphere, emotional extremity, and moral unease, then the film's achievement is substantial. It embraces the gothic not as a collection of stylistic markers, but as a worldview—one in which excess is not corrected, devotion is not moderated, and suffering is not required to justify itself through growth.

The film succeeds most clearly in reclaiming the gothic as a space of seriousness. It refuses irony and resists modernization through simplification. Instead of translating the myth into contemporary accessibility, it allows the gothic's severity to remain intact, even when that severity clashes with modern expectations of agency, balance, and redemption. This refusal gives the film a coherence that many reinterpretations lack. It knows what it is doing, and it does not dilute that purpose to broaden appeal.

As a reimagining, the film also succeeds in shifting the myth's center of gravity. Dracula is no longer defined primarily by threat or transgression, but by endurance. The horror is not invasion, but fixation. By reframing immortality as emotional stasis and love as ethical pressure rather than salvation, the film extends the myth into territory that feels both old and newly uncomfortable. It does not reinvent Dracula by adding novelty; it does so by staying too long with an idea earlier versions gesture toward and then abandon.

However, this success is conditional. The film's commitment to gothic logic means accepting its costs. Gothic narratives traditionally tolerate imbalance—of power, of voice, of consequence. In preserving this imbalance without corrective framing, the film risks reproducing the very dynamics it may be interrogating. Whether this is seen as artistic honesty or ethical limitation will differ from viewer to viewer.

The film succeeds, then, not as a universal reimagining, but as a rigorous one. It does not aim to reconcile gothic tradition with contemporary values. It allows them to collide and refuses to resolve the tension. In doing so, it restores the gothic's capacity to unsettle rather than reassure. If success is defined as provocation sustained with integrity, the film achieves it. If success requires accessibility, balance, or emotional release, it does not.

18.2 Strengths Versus Shortcomings

The film's greatest strengths are inseparable from its most significant shortcomings. Its seriousness, coherence, and emotional ambition give it weight, but they also limit its flexibility. The same qualities that grant the film identity are the ones that narrow its reach.

Among its strengths is its tonal discipline. The film maintains a unified emotional register from beginning to end, refusing to fracture itself for convenience. This discipline creates a sense of intentionality that carries through every aspect of the work—from pacing and performance to visual design and thematic focus. Few films commit so fully to their internal logic, and fewer still sustain that commitment without compromise.

The film's treatment of love as morally unstable rather than redemptive is another strength. It resists romantic immunity and subjects devotion to ethical scrutiny without resorting to didacticism. This approach deepens the myth and invites reflection rather than assent. It trusts the audience to grapple with discomfort rather than resolving it on their behalf.

Its willingness to deny catharsis is also a strength, though a contentious one. By refusing emotional release, the film preserves the integrity of its central condition. Endurance remains endurance. Nothing is softened retroactively. This refusal gives the film a rare coherence, even when it frustrates.

Yet these same choices produce the film's most apparent shortcomings. The pacing, while thematically aligned, can feel punishing. Duration does not always deepen meaning; at times, it merely extends it. Repetition risks dulling rather than sharpening emotional impact, particularly for viewers less inclined toward contemplative cinema.

The film's handling of agency—especially for supporting and female characters—remains ethically unsettled. While the narrative may intend to critique emotional domination, it does not always provide sufficient counterweight to prevent that domination from feeling structurally reinforced. The lack of narrative resistance can feel less like exposure and more like resignation.

There is also the question of emotional range. The film's severity allows little room for contrast. Without modulation, intensity can become monotone. Some viewers may experience this as rigor; others as emotional exhaustion. The film does not distinguish clearly between productive discomfort and diminishing return.

Ultimately, the balance between strength and shortcoming depends on one's tolerance for austerity. The film excels when judged on coherence, ambition, and seriousness. It falters when judged on accessibility, narrative generosity, or ethical clarity. It is not a work that fails through inconsistency, but one that risks failure through excess of conviction.

What remains undeniable is that the film knows what it is willing to sacrifice. It trades breadth for depth, consensus for integrity, and comfort for coherence. Whether those sacrifices feel justified will determine whether the film's strengths outweigh its shortcomings—or whether its shortcomings become inseparable from its achievement.

18.3 Lasting Impression and Critical Assessment

The lasting impression of Dracula: A Love Tale is not one of narrative satisfaction, but of sustained pressure. It is a film that does not recede easily into memory as a sequence of scenes or moments. Instead, it persists as a condition—an emotional and ethical atmosphere that lingers long after the final image has faded. What remains is not clarity, but weight.

Critically, this persistence is both the film's most admirable quality and its most challenging one. The work refuses to resolve itself into a verdict. It does not guide the viewer toward approval or rejection, nor does it soften its implications with reassurance. As a result, the film resists the usual categories of success or failure. It cannot be easily summarized as effective or ineffective, because its ambition lies outside efficiency.

What the film achieves most convincingly is coherence. Every formal decision—pacing, performance, visual restraint, thematic focus—aligns with its central preoccupation: endurance without transformation. There are no tonal contradictions, no late-stage reversals designed to appease discomfort. The film sustains its severity with discipline. This coherence gives it authority. Even viewers who reject its approach often recognize that it has been carried through with intention rather than accident.

From a critical standpoint, the film's seriousness is its defining trait. It does not hedge its ideas or seek validation through irony. In a cinematic landscape often marked by self-awareness and tonal hybridity, this earnestness feels almost defiant. The film assumes that emotional extremity can be examined without apology, and that ambiguity does not require resolution to be meaningful.

At the same time, this seriousness limits the film's elasticity. Its refusal to modulate tone or pace creates an experience that some will experience as rigorous and others as exhausting. The film asks much of its audience and offers little relief in return. For some critics, this imbalance undermines its effectiveness, suggesting that endurance alone is not sufficient to sustain engagement. For others, that very imbalance is the point—the ethical structure of the film mirrored in its form.

The film's critical legacy is likely to be shaped less by consensus than by division. It is the kind of work that generates essays rather than ratings, arguments rather than summaries. Its value lies in how it provokes thought rather than how it satisfies expectation. Over time, it may be revisited not because it is beloved, but because it remains unresolved.

Importantly, the film does not age itself through topical commentary. Its concerns—love without limit, grief without end, endurance mistaken for virtue—are not bound to a specific cultural moment. They recur across eras, just as the myth itself does. This gives the film a durability that is separate from popularity. It may never be widely embraced, but it is unlikely to be easily dismissed.

In assessing the film critically, it becomes clear that it does not aspire to completeness. It does not attempt to offer a definitive statement on Dracula, on romance, or on redemption. Instead, it positions itself as one sustained thought, carried as far as possible without contradiction. That thought is not comforting, but it is consistent.

The lasting impression, then, is not admiration in the conventional sense, but respect for conviction. The film stands by its choices even when those choices alienate. It accepts the cost of seriousness without seeking compensation. Whether one ultimately finds the experience rewarding or withholding, it is difficult to argue that it is careless.

Dracula: A Love Tale leaves behind an impression not of closure, but of insistence. It insists that love can be destructive without being insincere, that immortality can be punishment without spectacle, and that endurance can hollow meaning rather than preserve it. These ideas do not resolve themselves. They remain.

And in remaining—heavy, unresolved, and resistant to easy judgment—the film secures its place not as a definitive reimagining, but as a demanding one. A work that may not invite return, but that continues to ask for consideration long after it has ended.

Chapter 19 — Legacy and Long-Term Impact

19.1 How This Film May Be Remembered

Dracula: A Love Tale is unlikely to be remembered as a popular turning point or a definitive reinvention. Its afterlife will be quieter and more selective. It will persist less as a cultural reference point than as a work that lingers in critical memory, resurfacing whenever questions arise about how far a myth can be pressed before it resists resolution.

The film's most enduring quality is its refusal to simplify itself for remembrance. It does not offer a signature image or a singular moment designed to stand in for the whole. Instead, it leaves behind an atmosphere—one of emotional severity, ethical strain, and deliberate incompleteness. Viewers may forget details of plot or sequence, but they are less likely to forget the sensation of having remained with something that would not release them.

Over time, the film may be recalled as emblematic of a period in cinema when seriousness returned without irony, when filmmakers were willing to risk alienation in pursuit of coherence. It will likely be cited less for innovation than for endurance—for having sustained a single idea longer than comfort would allow. Its reputation will rest not on what it resolved, but on what it refused to resolve.

This kind of remembrance is not broad, but it is durable. The film may not inspire nostalgia, but it will invite reconsideration. It will be remembered by those who felt unsettled rather than satisfied, by viewers who sensed that the film asked more of them than it was willing to give back.

19.2 Its Place in the Dracula Canon

Within the long and varied Dracula canon, this film occupies a marginal but meaningful position. It does not replace earlier interpretations, nor does it attempt to synthesize them. Instead, it withdraws from the dominant narrative currents—horror, seduction, spectacle—and settles into a narrower channel defined by endurance and fixation.

Most canonical entries position Dracula as a force in motion: invading, corrupting, seducing, or being pursued. Even tragic versions rely on momentum. This film resists that structure. Dracula here is not a catalyst for action, but a condition that persists. The myth's usual tension between predator and society dissolves into a quieter conflict between memory and time.

As a result, the film will not sit comfortably alongside versions that emphasize fear, eroticism, or narrative propulsion. Its contribution to the canon is not additive in the sense of expanding lore or iconography. It is interrogative. It asks what remains of the myth when movement is removed, when love is allowed to dominate completely, and when immortality is treated as stasis rather than power.

In this way, the film functions as a kind of critical footnote to the canon—a sustained meditation rather than a reinterpretation meant for repetition. It will likely be referenced in discussions of Dracula as tragic figure rather than as monster, and in conversations about how myth behaves when stripped of resolution.

Its place in the canon is therefore not central, but clarifying. It does not define Dracula for future generations, but it sharpens one possible reading of him: not as a being who defies death, but as one who refuses change.

19.3 Final Thoughts on Its Cultural Significance

The cultural significance of *Dracula: A Love Tale* lies in its resistance to reassurance. At a moment when many stories aim to comfort, balance, or resolve, this film insists on severity. It challenges the assumption that love redeems by default, that suffering ennobles, or that endurance proves virtue. These challenges resonate beyond the confines of gothic romance.

Culturally, the film reflects a growing unease with absolutism—emotional, moral, or ideological. Its portrayal of love as something that can harm when denied limits speaks to contemporary conversations about boundaries, agency, and emotional entitlement. The film does not moralize these issues; it exposes their consequences through duration rather than argument.

Its significance also lies in its treatment of grief. By refusing to frame grief as a passage toward healing, the film acknowledges an experience many recognize but rarely see sustained onscreen. Grief here is not instructive. It does not resolve. It shapes identity over time. This portrayal resists cultural pressure to recover quickly or productively from loss.

Finally, the film's cultural role may be to remind audiences that not all myths are meant to be corrected. Some are meant to be endured, questioned, and left unresolved. In preserving discomfort rather than eliminating it, the film honors the darker function of myth: not to console, but to confront.

Dracula: A Love Tale may never be widely embraced, but its significance does not depend on consensus. It exists as a provocation carried through with discipline. Its contribution is not a lesson or a legacy of answers, but a sustained insistence that some stories matter precisely because they refuse to end cleanly.

In that refusal, the film secures its place—not as a definitive Dracula, but as a demanding one. A work that stands apart from its canon not by rejecting it, but by pressing one of its oldest questions to the point where endurance itself becomes the subject.

Chapter 20 — Afterword

20.1 Why *Dracula: A Love Tale* Will Continue to Be Discussed

Dracula: A Love Tale will continue to be discussed not because it resolves anything, but because it refuses to. Its endurance in cultural conversation will mirror the endurance it depicts—persistent, unresolved, and resistant to closure. The film does not settle into a stable interpretation, and that instability is precisely what keeps it alive.

Discussion will persist because the film occupies a space that criticism itself struggles to categorize. It is neither comfortably romantic nor conventionally tragic, neither fully condemnatory nor quietly redemptive. Each viewing reopens questions rather than answers them. Viewers return not to confirm what they felt before, but to test whether their discomfort has shifted. Often, it has not.

The film also invites debate because it challenges deeply ingrained narrative assumptions. It resists the belief that love must justify suffering, that endurance must lead somewhere, or that awareness must redeem. These refusals do not align neatly with dominant cinematic ethics. As a result, the film becomes a reference point whenever conversations arise about emotional absolutism, moral ambiguity, or the limits of empathy.

Its continued discussion is also ensured by its relationship to myth. Dracula is a figure perpetually rewritten, and each version implicitly argues with those that came before it. This film enters that argument without attempting to win it. Instead, it isolates one thread—love without finitude—and pulls until the fabric strains. Future reinterpretations will either react against this severity or build upon it. Either way, this version remains part of the conversation by virtue of how far it went.

Finally, the film will persist in discourse because it divides without collapsing. Polarization often fades when one side exhausts itself. Here, disagreement remains productive. The film does not invite dismissal. It invites return. Its questions age slowly, because they are not tied to topical reference but to enduring human tension: how long devotion can last before it becomes harm.

20.2 Closing Reflections on Love, Myth, and Cinema

In its final reckoning, *Dracula: A Love Tale* offers no comfort about love, no reassurance about myth, and no apology about cinema's capacity to unsettle. What it offers instead is insistence. It insists that love is not inherently redemptive, that myths do not exist to soothe, and that cinema can function as an ethical pressure rather than an emotional release.

Love, as the film presents it, is neither false nor pure. It is sincere, intense, and devastating in equal measure. Its danger lies not in its weakness, but in its refusal to change. The film suggests that love requires mortality—not only to begin, but to remain humane. When love survives death unchanged, it loses proportion. It ceases to be relational. It becomes possession.

Myth, in this context, is not a relic to be modernized, but a structure to be tested. The film does not correct the Dracula myth by updating its values. It confronts the myth with its own logic and allows that logic to reach exhaustion. In doing so, it reveals that myths endure not because they resolve human contradiction, but because they preserve it.

Cinema, finally, is treated not as spectacle or consolation, but as duration. The film trusts time as its primary tool. It believes that remaining with an idea—without softening it, without escaping it—can produce understanding that explanation cannot. This is a demanding vision of cinema, one that assumes viewers are willing to endure ambiguity rather than be guided around it.

These closing reflections do not point toward synthesis. Love remains ethically unstable. Myth remains unresolved. Cinema remains demanding. The film does not reconcile these forces because reconciliation would betray its central insight: that some truths do not arrive as answers, but as conditions we must learn to recognize.

Dracula: A Love Tale ends where it began—with endurance. Not as virtue, not as triumph, but as fact. What it asks, finally, is not whether love can last forever, but what forever does to love when it refuses to end.

That question does not conclude with the film. It continues—in criticism, in debate, and in the uneasy silence that follows stories unwilling to release us.